Thumbs up for *What*

Marc MacYoung and Jenn
be covered in all self-defer ... Sadly, many of these issues are often trivialized or omitted. You owe it to yourself and your students if you instruct, to read and incorporate the lessons contained in "What You Don't Know Can Kill You." The information may keep you out of a civil courtroom, prison, or the morgue.

—Alain Burrese, J.D.,
Active Shooter Response Instructor and author of
Survive a Shooting

Far too often, authors mistakenly approach the subject of violence from the top-down. In "What You Don't Know Can Kill You," MacYoung and Meek give the novice an invaluable foundation for critical, analytical thought to a highly complex issue, and great cause for re-thinking strategy and tactics for the seasoned warrior.

—Liam Jackson
Former counter-terrorism SME, DoJ/DoD, and
LEO close-quarter combat instructor

Read this book, it'll do you good. Why? For several reasons including that you must know about the vital, life-altering, judicial side of self-defense.

Too many look at self-defense as purely physical actions. Others claim that paying too much attention to the legal side will make you freeze when it is imperative that you act. Too many spout moronic clichés like the hackneyed "tried by twelve... carried by six" phrase without realizing that the fight afterword will be longer, more arduous, and possibly more damaging than the actual incident. This book will show you why those responses are insufficient and boil a huge subject down to a mere and insufficient soundbite.

You need so much more to claim self-defense than to cry "I was in fear for my life!" The authors introduce you to what is needed to successfully defend yourself in the streets and court. Court is a place where words don't mean what you think or have learned, and opinion and political desire affect more things than justice does.

Why is that important? Because as is explained so well in this book by Marc and Jenna self-defense is purely a legal construct, a plea made after a traumatic incident has occurred. And it is a side of the self-defense paradigm that does not get enough attention. It does you no good to successfully defend your life and then get hung in the legal aftermath. And this book will inform you of the four important aspects of dealing with the judiciary.

Street people and criminals learn these things through experience. Save yourself the time, money, hassle, and free vacations to dingy and barred places by being smarter than we were. Learn from informed and educated writing.

In an easy to read understandable manner, using stories that you can relate to Jenna and Marc shed light on this important topic. Read it all the way through, read it in sections, then give it as a gift to others you care about so they too can learn this information.

—Terry Trahan
Director KSMA, Weasel Craft, and Masters of Mayhem

WHAT YOU DON'T KNOW CAN KILL YOU

How Most Self-Defense Training Will Put You into Prison or the Ground

Marc MacYoung
Jenna Meek

For permission to use this book contact:
Carry On Publishing
590 W Hwy 105, Suite 284
Monument, CO 80132
Publishing@CarryOnColorado.com

Cover design: Dan LoGrasso
Interior design: Jenna Meek, Carry On Publishing
Edited by: Dianna Gordon
Carry on Publishing/No Nonsense Self-Defense

First Edition, also available as an ebook
ISBN-13: 978-0-692-13053-7
ISBN-10: 0-692-13053-5

A man who knows and knows that he knows is wise; follow him.
A man who knows but knows not that he knows is lost;
show him the way.
A man who knows not but knows that he knows not is a child;
teach him.
A man who knows not but knows not that he knows not is a fool;
shun him.
Persian Proverb

Self-defense is more than just the ability to do it.
Far more important is to know when to act—and when not to.
That's a skill many wrongfully assume they already have.
Marc MacYoung

Many don't understand self-defense is so much more than just pulling the trigger—that's almost the easy part—the aftermath is a beast unto itself. It will last longer and be harder than the actual incident.
Are you prepared for the next fight of your life?
Jenna Meek

We hear people in the self-defense world wax poetic on how they are "the good guy" and assume the law will see it that way. Maybe, maybe not.

Who this book is for

Everyone who trains or who has trained in a self-defense program. Every single self-defense program, martial arts style, and firearms training you've had or are taking is on the table.

In just a minute, we will give you the four components of self-defense (SD). These must be addressed if you want to stay out of prison or the morgue. Self-defense is a big subject intertwined with many smaller topics. We want you to grasp the entire picture that makes up effective self-defense. Your safety and freedom are based on a general understanding of the full spectrum. The lack of any one of these four is dangerous.

Understand most training goes into great depths of one component. Where this specialization becomes a problem is the deeper you get into one the easier it becomes to ignore other components. The trap is how easy it is to tell yourself a deep and narrow focus is all you need. In your current training you may get one or maybe more of these components, but we've never seen all four fully addressed in one school.

There's no such thing as one-stop shopping for your self-defense needs. To get all these components, you have to look for them. This book is an introduction to what to look for.

Try to answer this question: What single component or limited combination were you taught?

The answer is: We don't know and odds are neither do you. (When you see the components take a minute and figure out which of them your training spotlighted and what it didn't.) But there's a bigger problem: If you are unaware of these components you are at the mercy of your training. Why's that a problem? You will be the one on the hook for what you do—not your instructors. You can't put responsibility on someone else for your actions.

Now that you know these four components exist you can take control of your education.

How do you do that? Keep reading.

Contents

The problem with soundbite self-defense
is how complete it sounds during training
and how fast it will put you into prison
or the cemetery if you use it.

Introduction

This primer is an introduction to the areas where things commonly go wrong with self-defense and self-defense claims. And when we say self-defense we mean it as a whole not any specific part of it.

It's easy to forget, there is a difference between self-defense and training for self-defense. What we are about to say applies to self-defense—not training. We said earlier there are four components of self-defense. They are:

1. Understanding violence
2. Mental preparation (including ethics on use)
3. Physical skills
4. Aftermath (legal and other issues)

Have you ever heard it put so simply? It's not… really. Each of those components is an ocean unto itself where you can dive into its depths—to the point of spending all your time there. What we can tell you is most training falls exclusively into one component (e.g., physical) or in predictable combinations (e.g., mental and physical). Whatever the reasons for doing so, this comes at the expense of other important information.

While you can count on those four components to be present in a self-defense incident, you can't rely on their being covered in your self-defense 'training.' The bad news is the disconnect between *what you get in training* and *what you'll need* is why you'll end up behind bars or maimed.

So do us a favor: Check what you already know about self-defense at the door. Throughout this book we'll cover what self-defense (as a whole) is, when to use your skills, and why you'll need to explain later how what you did was *necessary for defending yourself.* We will treat self-defense as the big picture from beginning to end. This might be different from what your last instructor taught you. After you read this book go back and reconcile the new information with the old. You'll be surprised when you find the differences and connections you've never seen before. A bit of advice about reading this book. Read it in small chunks, don't try to blaze through in one sitting. Give the ideas in a chapter some time to percolate. After a few months come back and reread it to see how your understanding has changed.

That brings us to soundbite self-defense training. What is soundbite training? It is when component-specific information is presented as *all you need to know* about self-defense. It basically presents one piece of the puzzle as the whole picture. This not to say the information is incorrect or unimportant, but it is still only one element of a particular component. Typically this exclusive focus is physical, but not always. Here's the hitch; to understand the bigger picture you have to push the limits of your comfort zone. Soundbites often lull you into not learning about those other important topics.

Soundbite training's emphasis on one aspect of self-defense often mixes with the gross oversimplification of other components and dismissal—if not outright ignorance—of still other factors. To maintain the delusion you understand self-defense, serious and complex issues are reduced to soundbites (e.g., "I'd rather be judged by twelve than carried by six" and "In a real fight, I'd…"). It's an invisible problem, but soundbite self-defense has the recognizable sound of minds not just closing but slamming shut.

A real-world problem comes with that attitude. To explain it, we'll use an analogy. Soundbite self-defense training is like a bullet-proof vest you don't know is faulty. It will give you confidence that lasts right up until it fails *at the worst possible moment*. Overconfidence in limited training can prompt you to walk into situations you really should avoid. We've seen it happen—up to the point of people dying.

Worse is the mental lock-up and physical freeze when things go sideways in a manner you don't expect. It's the fist that crashes through your block; the mugger who unexpectedly appears next to you because—despite your 'situational awareness'—he stood where you didn't know to look. (And you didn't know because, with all the time you spend to learn to handle a robbery, nobody ever explains how robberies are committed); or dropping the gun you're trying to 'quickdraw.'

All of this is not your fault, but it *is* your problem.

Ordinarily you wouldn't know what your training lacked until it was too late. Changing analogies, it's like a tire that unexpectedly blows out. It can happen anywhere along the way—including after you've 'won' the physical part of 'self-defense.' The question is will that tire failure put you in the hospital, the ground, or jail? The answer is—that "it depends on *where* the flaw is and *when* it goes." This is part of what Marc means when he says, "You'll have only one of two problems with using your self-defense training. One, it doesn't work. Two, it does work."

We cannot stress enough that you can't be expected to know things that aren't covered in your training. These things exist in the real world, however, and—if you act—they *will* come into play. You will be the one who suffers for not knowing them—not your school, not your teacher, *you*. That's not a threat it's just how things work. It's about as predictable as what happens if you try to walk across the desert in summer without protective gear and water—and about as personal.

Stripped of their veneers, martial arts and firearms training teach you how to harm another person. But society and the legal system have some definite 'opinions' about you doing that. There's enough instruction out there on the physical parts of self-defense so we're not going to spend much time on it. (There's a lot of instruction on "how" so we'll spend time on "when" and "how much.") We're going to invest more time on the other topics that aren't as fun and sexy. These topics deal with how society and the cops will react to your defending yourself. Honestly, has your previous training covered them? Or does the dominant attitude contend that "it will obviously be self-defense, so let's focus on the physical part"? No matter how much force you're being taught to use.

At the same time, you can use this book as a litmus test to determine how good your training has been. It's a good sign if you're already familiar with many of the points we talk about. Better yet you can use this primer as a diagnostic tool to establish what you need to look into. You can also use it to decide if where you currently put your money really does help with your self-defense goals.

We're going to warn you right now: Self-defense is both more narrow *and* a lot larger subject than you imagine. Stepping into this new definition can be intimidating and confusing. It doesn't have to be. Jenna and her husband Jeff are firearms instructors. She sums it up this way, *It's a pendulum effect. We see people come in for entry-level classes usually because the state mandates they need minimal training to get a concealed carry permit.*

Afterward the result is commonly a confident feeling of "I've got this whole self-defense thing." That and the false idea that because you've never been on the wrong side of the law means that you never will be is the pendulum swinging all the way to one side. When we get students back who want more training if they are presented with the legal aspects of self-defense the mood change is often ""oh my God! I can get arrested for anything! Maybe this isn't for me after all!" or worse ""if this is the cost of defending myself maybe that's a little too much".

That's the pendulum swinging to the opposite side. Neither of these are good places for a person's mind and attitude to be. Where we ultimately want people is in the middle. Yes, there is a lot involved, but it is manageable. If you are well versed, prepared, and have a good working understanding of what's involved the pendulum stops its swing and ends up in the middle. When people's minds are there, they have a balance between the two extremes—that allows them to have both personal safety and a normal everyday life.

One of our goals is to help you gain control of the pendulum swing. We won't go into these topics in depth, but we will cover a wide range of topics you might want to look into at your own pace. Our main goal is far more pragmatic. If you are ever in a situation where you have to defend yourself, this prior knowledge will help you navigate the realities of violence and its aftermath. It won't be all rainbows and unicorns—but you'll have the tools to get through it with the least amount of stress and blood.

You ready? Then it's time to meet a new friend.

Tyler Story, One

Tyler is well trained in self-defense. He's spent years and thousands of dollars on training and equipment. With his emphasis on the physical, he's pretty sure he can handle himself. Tyler and his girlfriend, Brittany live on a street that ends at a park, three doors away. Late one Saturday night, they hear a disturbance in the park. Looking down the street he sees two groups facing off. He decides to go break up the situation. Seeing that there are about ten people, Tyler decides he better take a weapon along just in case. As he goes back in the house Brittany asks, "What's going on?" Tyler tells her he's going to the park. Brittany tells him to stay, but Tyler gets his 'toy,' sticks it in his pants and heads out to tell the groups to take their quarrel elsewhere.

Arriving at the park Tyler discovers two mixed groups of teenage males and females. Males from both groups have squared off and there's a confrontation between two of them. Believing his age will give him authority, Tyler demands to know what is going on. Initially they ignore him, so Tyler steps up and gets louder. Unfortunately a third guy tells Tyler to back off. Pissed off now, Tyler tells everyone he lives here and they need to leave his neighborhood. This doesn't go over well and when the kid's response has to do with Tyler's sexual practices with his mother, Tyler steps forward and shoves the younger man and demands they leave. The situation explodes into violence.

In the melee, Tyler pulls his self-defense item and uses it just as the cops roll up. Tyler and everyone else find themselves looking down the barrels of not only pistols but a rifle. Everyone is told to get down and spread their arms and legs. They lie there waiting for more police to arrive. After their arrival, everyone is immediately riot cuffed (hands zip tied together behind them) and searched. Tyler's item is taken and put into an evidence bag. When an officer interviews him, Tyler claims "self-defense." The officer asks if he left his property to come to the park. Tyler says, "Yes." Long story short, Tyler is arrested, taken to the station and charged with attempted murder. His defense bills run ten thousand dollars that he has to borrow from his parents. The lawyer gets his case pleaded down to aggravated assault. It's a slam dunk for the prosecution. Tyler spends a year in county jail and when he gets out, Brittany has left him, he has no job and he has to move back in with his parents.

To his dying day Tyler remains convinced he went to jail for defending himself.

Tyler has just learned the hard way that even though he's a good guy, he still made bad self-defense and use of force decisions. Refusing to occasionally and honestly reevaluate our convictions can lead us to a different kind of conviction.

*Self-defense doesn't mean what you think it means.
And it doesn't mean what most instructors say it does.
It especially doesn't mean what some twit on the Internet writes.
Self-defense is a legal term. In that context, it has
very strict standards and limits. Standards you must meet
and limits you must stay within—because you will be
held accountable to them. These standards are not the death
sentence many say, but not meeting them will ensure
a prison sentence.*

Shifting Gears

Let's talk about how to stay out of the hospital (or worse, the morgue) for failing to successfully defend yourself, as well as, not going to prison for successfully defending yourself. The two topics are very intertwined.

To not end up like our buddy Tyler (or in the hospital), there are five necessary 'shifts of your mental gears' that you have to make. These paradigm shifts run much deeper than the 'what's the best caliber' or 'what's the best martial art style' arguments you commonly hear in self-defense circles. Since neither the emergency room nor prison is where you want to end up—it's time to learn how to drive a mental stick shift.

- First gear: What is the incident?
- Second gear: Jack of all trades; master of none
- Third gear: Soundbite answers and clichés are wrong
- Fourth gear: "It depends" is usually the right answer.
- Fifth gear: Mental over physical skills

First: What *is* the incident?

Most people think of an incident as physical (e.g., the pull of the trigger or a punch). So that's where they invest their time and training. Let's face it, that's the fun part. Plus it's gratifying. Advancement and improvement in physical training are easily seen. The physical, however, is only a small part of self-defense. While 'being able to do' is important, exclusively focusing on it is an express ticket to the hospital or jail.

Let's say any self-defense incident has three stages:

- What happens before the violence
- The physical violence
- What happens afterward

Reading them laid out like that it might seem they're distinct parts. In truth they're as mixed up as a plate of spaghetti—but to introduce the idea it helps to break the process of violence into these simple parts.

That may not sound like much, but it's a massive paradigm shift. Same incident, different stages, radically different tactics, rules, emphasis, mindsets and goals in each stage. If you think the whole of the incident as just the physical part, you'll be unprepared for the other two. If your goal is not to be hospitalized or imprisoned, you'll need to know how to conduct yourself in *all* three stages.

Now ask yourself, how much of your training has been focused on the action instead of the when, why, how much and what happens next of self-defense? Or are you and the instructor just assuming you'll know when to use force? How much force to use? When to stop? Do you want to end up in prison? Because *not* knowing these is how you end up imprisoned for using your training.

Second: Jack of all trades; master of none.

With your new and expanded understanding of self-defense incidents comes the need for knowledge about issues other than the physical component. While that may sound like an unfair burden, you don't have to be an expert on every aspect of self-defense and its related fields. But if you ever find yourself in a situation where you might have to use your training you do have to know *a little about a whole lot*. You use that wide spectrum of knowledge to guide your actions for the best results and to avoid common mistakes.

Let us ask you the following:

- Do you know how violence happens? We mean in real life and not what you see in the movies.
- Do you know how violent crimes are committed? Again, not the Hollywood version.
- Do you know how to de-escalate a situation?

- Do you know what actions you can take to deter a potential attacker?
- Do you know de-escalation and deterrence are two different things?
- Do you know what actions will provoke someone to attack you—even if you are armed?
- Do you know how those points apply to whether or not you can even claim self-defense in court?
- Do you know the legal parameters of self-defense?
- Do you know those lines change depending on the circumstances? (The *exact* same move is self-defense in one situation and a crime in another.)
- Can you tell if someone is drunk or high by how he or she moves?
- Do you know how to explain the difference between a normal movement and an action that is a set up for an attack?
- Do you know how to scale the level of force you use?
- Can you spot a developing rape or robbery?

If you know these, odds are good you can keep from having to go physical to stay safe. If you still have to act, being able to explain what you did and why you did it are critical to keep from being convicted of a crime—even if you were acting in self-defense. Again, you don't have to have a master's degree in of all these, but as you'll soon see, a passing knowledge of them will do wonders to keep you out of prison for defending yourself.

Third: Soundbites and clichés are *overwhelmingly* wrong.

Do you know the difference between a complicated and a complex system? A watch is a *complicated system*. It takes multiple little parts working together to keep time. Thing is—they're all watch pieces put together in a way that works to keep time.

A *complex system* has a large number of factors influencing each other in a nonlinear way. (It's not just complicated, but it's multi-variant.) In complex systems cause doesn't always equal effect. Another part of the complexity is different things combine to create results that change—given the presence or absence of others. (Think cooking with spices.) Still another part that's wobbly is while a variable *will* be present in a certain type of situation (e.g., a robbery), the exact details are variable (e.g., how a particular robbery is attempted). Sometimes details change *as it's happening*. Your legally allowed options can vary within a matter of feet or by which direction a would-be attacker turns. *Wait,* there's more. Not only are things hard to predict in complex systems, but often—because of unknown factors—if you push something here, something completely unexpected pops up over there. Want another level of complexity? Your actions *will* influence what happens.

Self-defense is not a *complicated* problem, it is a *complex* issue. Success lies in shifting your thinking so you can function in complex conditions. What are the complexities? What are things you won't know until a situation occurs? Here's a short list:

- Where will it happen?
- How many attackers will there be?
- Will they be armed?
- Will you be alone or with someone?
- What will you be doing when those circumstances arise?
- How distracted are you?
- How much of the situation are you aware of in that instant?
- Are there important variables you are unaware of?
- Does your training apply to the level of situation you're in?

Then there are invisible factors. Not only is it impossible to predict how someone will try to rob you, but you *won't know*—until afterward—if the guy you had to defend yourself against was just a junkie or the little brother of the local gang-leader. (Vendettas are a problem when it comes to violence.) You *won't know* if it was filmed. You *don't* know if the police department that responds to the location has an unofficial '*someone* has to go to jail' policy. (It can sometimes be harder for a patrol officer not to arrest someone and then explain that decision to his superiors than to make a weak arrest.) You *don't* know how much discretion is allowed to the investigating officer. (He may already be under orders from the district attorney's [DA's] office to arrest you.) You *can't know* if the mayor has ordered a crackdown this month. Never thought about those last points? Such unseen forces often influence the decision to arrest. And once an arrest has been made, 'the legal machine' is put into gear.

All of that is background is needed to understand why soundbites and clichés *don't* work when it comes to self-defense. There is no way a soundbite can possibly cover all the variables and necessary knowledge.

Here's the problem when it comes to things that don't *normally* affect us: People tend to like simple, soundbite, *this-is-how-it-is* and *you-just-do-this* answers. And that applies to more than self-defense. These simplistic summations organize and help us to get through our day with the least amount of fuss. Soundbite positions let us say we 'know it' and move on to something we consider more important. We often tell ourselves we don't need to know more until we *do need* more knowledge. And by then it's too late. Ordinarily this isn't much of a problem, but is that the approach you want to take with your life, your health, the financial future of your family and a possible prison term? Those are the stakes when you have to defend yourself.

Here's the tricky part, sometimes—given a specific set of circumstances—a soundbite *is* a good starting point. The key part of that last sentence is 'starting point.' Yes there were qualifiers like 'sometimes' and 'given,' but the bigger issue is the soundbite is a beginning. It *isn't* a conclusion. Another way to look at it is a soundbite is a direction, when what you'll need is a compass. Yet this partial credibility (and the tendency to validate what they think they know) is what keeps soundbites entrenched in people's minds and alive in bad training.[1]

At its absolute best a soundbite is a rule of thumb; it's *not* a get out (or stay out) of jail free card. *Sometimes* it can keep you from making common mistakes when you don't have a full understanding of the subject. It's when you accept the soundbite as all- you- need- to- know- about- the- subject or base your entire strategy on it that it'll come back and bite you in the butt. It also won't help you if you screw up in other ways (e.g., what you did wasn't self-defense). In those circumstances, you've torpedoed your chances of an acquittal because you didn't bother to learn anything past the soundbite.

Take for example thinking all you have to say is "I was in fear for my life." Do you honestly think a prosecutor hasn't heard

---

1. What we often see about this looks like "my neighbor's uncle's friend is a cop and my neighbor told me, 'All I have to do is drag the dead guy into my home.'" This plus a four-hour class on carrying concealed weapons (ccw) with an incompetent instructor plus a five-minute YouTube video confirming previous information means, "Now I'm officially done learning, and I know all there is to know about SD."

that before—and knows how to blow it out of the water? (Hint. Ask Raul Rodriguez[2] of Texas. He infamously armed himself before leaving his property, then videoed himself walking down to engage in an altercation with his neighbors. While on the phone with 911, he is heard telling the dispatcher "my life is in danger now" and "these people are going to go try and kill me." Rodriguez then said, "I'm standing my ground here," and fatally shot his neighbor and wounded his two friends. Rodriguez is now serving life in prison. He knew all the clichés to spout, he just didn't know what *not* to do.)

In other cases, soundbites can become self-fulfilling prophecies. An example "expect to get cut." When a knife is involved expecting to be cut will usually result in you charging straight into a weedwhacker.

That's why we say soundbites are usually wrong—because *they aren't enough*. But you won't know it until it's too late. That's when you'll find out soundbite answers—like "I'd rather be judged by twelve than carried by six," "shut up and lawyer up, "or "you just ..."—are a fast track to prison.

Fourth: "It depends" is usually the right answer.

With complex issues, the 'right' answer is usually situationally specific. That's because presence or absence factors are what determine the appropriate answer to the situation.

Take for example someone coming at you and screaming "I'm going to kill you!" Do you shoot? If it's a six-four, 250-pound biker, you have good reason to believe him. But what if it's an eight-year-old? Or someone in a wheelchair? What if that person in the wheelchair has a knife? What about a gun? Is the person in the same room and charging? Or is he or she standing across the street? What about walking toward you from across the same street?

Now while these sound like silly examples, developing the ability to process information this way is fundamental for making good use of force decisions—including if you have to use force at all. As violence professional and self-defense instructor, Randy King says, "Violence is high-speed problem solving" This is a truth that many in training don't yet understand. (Unfortunately that applies to both trainees and many trainers as well.) Does your training teach you to—as Marc says—"Do the math"? And *do it in time?*

---

2. https://www.courtlistener.com/opinion/4264154/raul-rodriguez-v-state/

Sometimes you only have seconds to decide how much force to use. A decision that can save you, bury you, or put you into prison. Making the right decision requires you learn to 'think' this way *before* you find yourself in a physical situation.

Fifth: Pre-existing knowledge, assessment, and articulation over physical skills.

Yeah, yeah originally it was "mental over physical skills." That was an introduction, this is more accurate.

First things first: Pre-existing whut? Pre-existing knowledge is also known as prior knowledge. What applicable training, experience, research, or understanding did you have *before* the incident? In layman's terms, *how* did you know the danger was real? It's a lot more than "well everyone knows..."

So, by now you've noticed that the decisions you make before physical violence occurs are important. But why is the ability to communicate so important for the aftermath? Because the odds are good you will have to justify your actions to the authorities.

Notice the use of the word justify. We're not talking about just saying, "It was self-defense." By justify we mean you explain—and prove—what you did was indeed self-defense. Or getting into legal argle-bargle describing how circumstances warranted the level of force you used. That requires a whole lot more than you currently realize.

There's a fundamental truth about self-defense most people don't recognize until it punches them in the face. That is somebody is *always* going to be unhappy with your use of force decision. Often, demands for you to justify your action come from the same people who are unhappy with you. In fact, your ability to explain your actions helps you think of what is happening as an interrogation, not an interview. They're doing *everything* in their power to trip you up, nitpick your actions, undermine your assessment and decisions, make you doubt yourself, fumble, confess to a crime, or sell the jury that what you did *wasn't* self-defense.

And most people—because they haven't shifted mental gears—*will help them do that.* This is especially true if you had to resort to a higher level of force. We'll start out with higher use of force decisions and work our way back. Not because it's macho or tactikool, but because coming from that direction makes it easier to understand the importance of many of the concepts in this book (you know like how not to go to prison for defending yourself.)

With those five paradigm shifts in mind let's look at some points about what you're *not* being told by your instructors *in* and *about* your training.

First, there's a world of difference between training and the reality of an actual self-defense situation. Unfortunately, many have come to believe that training and experience is the same thing. No.

Second, training doesn't 'teach' you what to do in a situation. It helps you ingrain certain attributes you'll *need* to defend yourself. The key word in that last sentence is 'ingrain.' That's not only having the ability to effectively do it in a situation but without much conscious thought. That's important because you'll only have so much conscious 'brain power' in a situation. Under those circumstances there are problems you *really* need to focus your conscious thoughts on; you don't want to waste your thoughts on trying to figure out how to apply (or fix) your technique.

Third—a great deal of training is consumer-driven instead of focusing on preparing you for an incident. This pandering to the market actually sets you up for failure. That's because it gives people what they want not what they need. Until you know why it's important, learning what you need is boring. That's why so many training programs skip it.

Take your current training and hold it up to the standards of retired United Kingdom (UK) police officer and security consultant Martin Cooper. His observation is to 'win' in a self-defense incident you must do it on five fronts:

- You must be able to act.
- You must stop the attacker.
- You must be cleared of all criminal charges.
- You must 'win' in civil court.
- You must be able to emotionally handle the aftermath.

With your current training how many have been addressed? Our aim is to prepare you for all of them. We're not writing about 'if it happens' we want to equip you for '*when it happens.*'

We're often asked by students what will it look like when I am in a self-defense situation? Reading between the lines it seems like the question they are really asking is how will the situation unfold. We can't begin to answer this, but we can give you standards to recognize dangerous circumstances so you can spot them as they develop no matter how they manifest. That's an important skill to have before and after the physical response to an incident. (Remember first gear?) *Before* because that's how you're going to meet Martin's number one and two criteria. Three through five are important for *after*. Does your current training address these points?

Before you answer yes let's put this in perspective. As author and former LEO (law enforcement officer) Liam Jackson so succinctly put it: *I had this discussion with a local prosecutor in an area with a highly disparate violent crime rate. He said that in nearly every case of self-defense that he's examined over the past decade, the defendant began his or her statement with "I was afraid for my life." (And we're on board with this from personal experience.) He went on to say that in several cases defendants admitted that they learned the phrase from TV and it was the only thing that would keep them from being charged. So the prosecutor said his next question would be, "WHY?" He said about half of the defendants would shrug or just stare at him with blank expressions. Even in the cases in which self-defense was legitimate.*

The 'justice system' is a three-headed bear
and Joe Citizen is a wounded moose.
Not totally defenseless, but without a herd
around him it ain't looking good.
Liam Jackson

Court

So what happened to Tyler? First, what he did was not self-defense. But before we get to why let's look at the meat grinder his actions threw him into.

Courts serve an important purpose. They help keep bad people off the streets. While we may sound jaded the problem with claiming self-defense is you have to know how to work *within* the system to keep it from working *against* you. Not all the cops, judges, and prosecutors, are out to get you. But it's easy for them to view self-defense cases as you lying to cover your illegal violence—because that's what happened in the last ten cases they dealt with. We've seen it happen, and that's why we're cranky.[3] So please bear with us if our opinions show now and then.

If you're looking for 'justice' you've come to the wrong place. There are important distinctions and points for understanding how our court systems work.

1. *Ours is not a justice system.* Ours is a legal system. It's about what the laws say and how they are interpreted. This includes how your case applies to the law, *not* the other way around. Think of the law as a test that your case will be run through to see if it passes. A very brutal test in that once the machine is put into gear, it must run its course.

2. *Ours is an adversarial system.* While we recommend you look up that term, the short version is two sides slug it out to sell 'what happened' to a third party (a judge or jury). The goal of both sides is to *win*. Even though it's supposed to be about determining 'the truth' often both sides run over what actually

3. Speaking of our opinion showing... If we didn't care about people's lives being ruined by violence, we wouldn't be cranky. Nor would we have taken the time or effort to write this book.

happened in the race to win. *This is not like watching a movie* (where the audience sees the story unfold). The jury depends entirely on what's told to them. It also happens to be told by two parties with bias. Long before they're ever seated, there's been a fight between lawyers about what the jury will be allowed to know about your case and what will be kept from the record. One side is fighting to keep out evidence that will convict you; the other is fighting against evidence that will exonerate you. So don't go in thinking 'the truth will protect you.' That is *not* enough.

3. *The system runs on money and metrics.* This point is like gravity: You don't see it, but it has a major influence on everything. First, the money. Our system costs a lot of money and it makes a bunch more. How much? By itself, prison labor (inmates providing low-cost labor) is estimated to be a billion dollar a year industry.[4] That isn't a slice of the pie, it's just a forkful. Including the lawmakers, police, courts, prisons, and lawyer fees, we're talking *hundreds* of billions being made and spent. That kind of money is not thrown around without metrics. Metrics? That's a business tool to measure performance and results. The combination of money and metrics have all kinds of unseen influences—including what is prosecuted. For example, a district attorney (DA) with an office that doesn't produce a high conviction rate won't keep his or her position for long. It's just common sense that when the boss's job is at stake, it affects the prosecutors working for him or her. Same goes for police and investigations. Arrests indicate they're doing their jobs. If they don't arrest, they're going to have to explain to their bosses why they weren't doing their jobs—which means their career is on the line. While a big arrest makes the news, a string of smaller—easier to prosecute—arrests keep the bosses happy. Don't think this doesn't affect who gets arrested. While the system is necessary, money and metrics can (and often do) shade into what is known in economics as perverse incentives[5]—especially when it comes to self-defense.

4. *Police and lawyers are professionals.* So too are many of the criminals they deal with. Being a professional is about more than getting paid. They have skills and are players in the game *they*

---

4. That's the lowball estimate. As there's no clear definition of the term, estimates vary between one and three billion—depending on whether the source is arguing for or against it.

5. Perverse incentives are when a rule, policy, or agenda has negative unintended consequences while encouraging these results due to the self-interest of those involved. At the same time, it is detrimental to the original goals. There are many types of perverse incentives. For example, raising taxes to the point where it behooves people to cheat on them.

understand and you—as a law-abiding citizen—don't. Law enforcement and DAs are good enough to catch and convict professional criminals. To successfully handle the aftermath of self-defense, you're going to need to be smart about it, and you'll (usually) need professional help.

5. *The system's original focus was on rights, not wrongs.* The Founding Fathers were big on protecting "rights." Some pretty clear standards were set. The courts had to meet them before they were allowed to strip people of freedom, life, and property. (If that still holds true is an argument beyond the scope of this book.) But look at it this way, the guy you just admitted hurting has rights, too. You will have to justify your reaction to the illegal violence he offered you. *If you can't, you've admitted to committing illegal violence on a fellow citizen.*

It may seem to you (a good guy) that you defended yourself against a 'bad guy,' but that's not how the law sees it. *Every* citizen has rights. The government and laws are supposed to protect those (sometimes from the government itself, sometimes from your fellow citizens). If you've acted in self-defense, you've injured—possibly killed—a fellow citizen. What you have to explain is how your fellow citizen offered you an unprovoked and sufficient threat to warrant what you did. As Massad Ayoob says, *The law doesn't see it as you versus a dirtbag. The law sees two citizens in dispute.* That's why you have to be prepared to be grilled like a cheese sandwich. (If you believe it will be obvious you were the good guy [and get offended at having to defend your actions] you've just shot yourself in the foot.)

6. *Most defense attorneys don't have a lot of experience—if any—representing actual self-defense cases.* This point will take some explanation, in fact lots of explaining. First, no we didn't just disrespect attorneys. Second, in no way did we say you're smarter than your attorney. You may know more about self-defense than your attorney, but attorneys know more about the law and legal system than you can imagine. Together you cover all the bases. Third, the 'self-defense' defense (no we didn't just stutter) automatically goes beyond being a soundbite or a cliché. the self-defense defense is what is known as an "affirmative defense."

What we're about to say will make lawyers squeal, but it's the easiest way for lay people to understand a critical idea. Ready? Claiming self-defense means you confess you *did* commit a crime (battery or even homicide), but you can provide enough good reasons for why you acted as you did, so you shouldn't be punished. This is the tricky part because it shifts the burden of proof to your team.

Now to soothe the lawyers' ruffled feathers, let's use the proper terms.

- You've admitted to the elements of a crime.
- Your side must argue you acted within legal allowances.
- The production of evidence is now your team's responsibility.

For everyone else, let's look at this in terms of workload. Ordinarily the task of the prosecutor is to prove—beyond a reasonable doubt—that you did it. Meanwhile, your side is saying you didn't. That you 'did it' is agreed by both sides when you claim self-defense. Now *you* have to be able to explain:

- Why given the circumstances you reasonably believed you were in immediate danger?
- You were not involved in the creation and escalation of the problem.
- You acted appropriately to the level of threat.

Your attorney must first present a strong enough argument to the judge so that the self-defense claim is allowed. Second, he or she must use that same evidence so the prosecutor *cannot* convince the jury what you did wasn't self-defense. Claiming self-defense puts the heavy lifting on your team.

This is radically different from the way defense attorneys normally operate. Typically claims of self-defense are an outright lie. Understand after some other dude did it (SODDI), 'self-defense' is the most common explanation for use of illegal violence. This comes in two forms.

The first type of self-defense isn't. Criminals commit violence on each other all the time—and they often get caught. Just as often the evidence against them is overwhelming. Figuring it's their only hope they claim 'self-defense.' From this moment on the best the attorney can do is damage control. Criminal violence is the largest percentage of so-called self-defense cases lawyers will handle.

The second type of 'self-defense' case attorneys deal with are *Tylers*. Someone who thinks he acts in self-defense steps outside the boundaries *of* SD.

Explanation time: Remember the first gear shift when thinking of a self-defense incident in three parts? Here's where it becomes critical. What you do in the first two stages will determine if it's actually self-defense *or not*. More specifically whether you'll be able to successfully claim self-defense. A term you need to look into is *imperfect self-defense*. For example, you may think you acted in self-defense, but arming yourself and leaving your property to confront someone on his property pretty much torpedoes your claim. (Remember Raul Rodriguez "pursuing a discussion of differences" with his neighbor? It bought him a life sentence.) This often is where attorneys and clients butt heads. You may be convinced that it's self-defense, but your attorney knows how the prosecution will tear your case apart. *If* you've stepped outside those boundaries you need to listen to your attorney.

Another reason actual self-defense is outside most lawyers' comfort zones is in SODDI your attorney picks apart the state's case. In self-defense cases it's reversed. In imperfect self-defense cases your lawyer will angle for damage control. In cases of *actual* self-defense your attorney has to help you defend your actions to the jury. Your side has to fight to prove *why* it was self-defense—even if your attacker died. Meanwhile the prosecutor will be nitpicking your version to sell the jury on why it wasn't self-defense. That's really unfamiliar territory for most attorneys. The following comment will make more sense after you've read the part about plea deals. But you need an attorney who knows how to defend you not just plea bargain.

Marty Hayes, JD, of The Armed Citizens Legal Defense Network, has this to say: *Virtually all defense attorneys are well-meaning, and truly want to do the best job for the client whether or not the client actually committed a crime or is one of the rare individuals who are actually innocent. But the law school experience fails most law students because the majority of law schools simply do not devote any time to defending the self-defense case. My experience in law school was about 90 minutes, and a good portion of that instruction was wrong, in my opinion, law schools do one thing and that is to prepare a person to pass the bar exam. If the student learns something about how to be an attorney along the way that is a bonus.*

So, how does one combat this? The reader must seek out an attorney who has studied the realm of self-defense law on their own, and then sit down with them beforehand and discuss the different issues ahead of time. Is this going to cost? Probably.

Though some attorneys are so passionate about self-defense they might spend an hour or so just educating a prospective client for no charge. Many of the attorneys associated with the Armed Citizens' Legal Defense Network are those kinds.

The one thing the self-defense client needs to understand is he or she will need to testify as to why he or she did what they did. The jury has the right to hear in your own words why you felt your life was in danger, and why you decided deadly force was your only reasonable option. Absent this, you will probably be convicted. And of course, there is no guarantee that just testifying will be enough. There are a lot of moving parts that go into a successful self-defense plea and acquittal. The first starts with your own education because a well-educated self-defense client is much easier to defend than the regular old gun club buddy who has never given this any thought.

Greg Hopkins an attorney, firearms instructor, and author of "A Time to Kill" has this story about law school: *The prof gave us an article from the local newspaper on a shooting and told us to tell how we'd handle it legally. The first three people he asked told how they would prosecute the case and assured us that it was a prosecution slam-dunk. The prof sighed, and asked, "Did anyone analyze this from the defense side?" Out of eighty-four students only I and one other raised our hands. He called on me. I hadn't gotten a minute into my take before there were hisses and derisive comments from the class. "Shut up!" commanded the prof. (He was a federal prosecutor, by the way) "You can't all be prosecutors! Most of your criminal work will be on defense, and Mr. Hopkins is showing you exactly how it should be defended!" But other than that day, we had zero instruction on defending a self-defense case*.

7. ***Law doesn't care if there's a danger—it cares if you can explain why you "reasonably believed..."***

This is another point that will take some explaining. First off, in case you haven't guessed it just claiming 'self-defense' or 'I was in fear for my life' *isn't* going to cut it.

Putting this in legal argle-bargle: You must also provide evidence of objective factors that led to a reasonable belief you were in immediate danger.

In plain English, you have to be able to point to *external* factors that made you believe you were about to be hurt. What did you see him do? Physical evidence is good, video is even better,[6]

6. Your statement has to match what shows up on security video.

witnesses verifying your story also are good. But in all cases, you must explain what was happening and *how* you knew it was dangerous—even if it wasn't.

Wait... what?

Among the anti-cop crowd there is a strong belief that the police get away with murder. Their shrieking reaches a pinnacle when an officer shoots someone who is unarmed. In defense of the police, often this comes down to what the individual was doing when the officer opened fire. While charging the officer is most common, a close second for getting shot by the police is a furtive movement. *a furtive movement... is a movement consistent with going for a weapon and not reasonably consistent with anything else under the circumstances* (Massad Ayoob).

Someone going for a concealed handgun can look like he's pulling up his shirt to show you his appendectomy scar. At a dinner party amongst friends, and discussing surgeries trying to show you his scar is understandable. In a lonely parking lot at night? Not so much. There it usually means he's going for a gun.

Pulling up your pants also can look like you're going for a gun. (That action got Daniel Shaver[7] killed by an Arizona police officer.) Is there a gun present? *It doesn't matter.* For their own survival police are trained to act during a critical incident if the suspect moves in a way that looks like he is reaching for a weapon. (If an officer has a gun on you immediately do—*and only do*—what he tells you. This goes double if you have a weapon.)

The reason for at the furtive movement is if the suspect *goes* for a gun the officer will be shot if he waits until he can see it. Knowing this, you'll view the Daniel Shaver shooting video[8] in a different light. Incidentally the police were responding to a call about a man with a gun. Even though Shaver was unarmed at the time of the shooting, the reason the officer was acquitted was due to his training and ability to explain why it was reasonable. It did look like Shaver was going for a gun.

In a non-shooting context there's a guy across the street, yelling that he's going to kick your butt. If you charge through traffic to engage, that isn't going to fly in court as self-defense. You can tell yourself you were defending yourself, but you've become the

---

7. https://bit.ly/2Bhy5qA

8. The call was about someone pointing 'a gun' from Shaver's fifth floor room at people in the pool. It would later be revealed Shaver was drunk as a skunk with a blood alcohol content (BAC) of .29 and it was a pellet rifle he used to kill birds.

aggressor. There wasn't an immediate danger until you closed the distance. 'Reasonably believes' must be based on conditions that make violence happening *to you* not just possible but probable within the next few seconds (immediate threat).

Later we will discuss not only how to make this determination, but also how to explain it in a way that strengthens your defense. While this seventh point might seem squishy and vague, it's an important foundation for many of the problems we'll talk about later.

8. *Civil versus criminal court.* This is a good news and bad news situation. The good news is the same tools and knowledge you use to steer clear of criminal charges will be major tools to help you 'win' in civil court. The bad news is civil proceedings differ from criminal court.

The differences start with the standards to have the ruling or verdict go for *or* against you. 'Beyond a reasonable doubt' is the criteria in criminal proceedings and 'preponderance of evidence' in civil (as low as fifty-one percent). 'Beyond' has been described as "more sure than not" while 'preponderance' is described as "more convincing evidence."

Another big difference is the state needs reasons, has financial constraints, and standards to prosecute. *Civilians don't.* Anybody can file a lawsuit against anyone, any organization, and even the government. While having a lawyer helps a person doesn't even need one to sue you. They can file the paperwork themselves. This is another 'once the machine is put into gear, the process must run its course.' We hope that the frivolous lawsuits will never see the light of day, but it will still take you time and money to get them thrown out. If your lawyer can't get the case thrown out, you have to ride it through until the bitter end.

While there are many legitimate cases, often civil lawsuits are akin to throwing spaghetti against the wall. The party bringing a civil suit is throwing whatever they can at you to see what will "stick" in court or more accurately to see how much they can take you for. You may have injured him or killed a loved one of theirs, and they want to make you pay. Literally.[9]

Civil courts also have their own versions of copping a plea. The civil attorney will research whether or not you are financially worth going after. *Judgment proof* is the lawyerly way of saying,

---

9 If you aren't charged criminally (or beat the criminal charges) the chances of you being sued increase. With some if he can't beat you physically or have you thrown in jail civil court is an alternative 'win.'

"You're not worth suing." It's when you are worth suing that what we're about to say comes into play. First, know that civil lawyers often work on 'spec'—that's to say they'll work for part of the settlement. So it's in their interest to sue the pants off you. Then know often cases will be settled in order to avoid the long, expensive, and arduous task of fighting to the bitter end.

The individual (or surviving family members) can try to sue you for defending yourself. This isn't just for medical expenses but also for the pain and suffering you inflicted on them. Being sued this way *really* sticks in the craw. You've survived being attacked, you've dealt with being interrogated by the cops, you've fought off criminal charges… and now this? That just piles insult on injury. Are you up for another fight? Or would it be easier to settle? This is something you need to seriously talk over with your civil attorney and family.

9. *Plea bargains.* Saying these are a trend in the criminal system is like claiming the Mississippi River is a drainage ditch. Remember ours is not a justice system, but a legal one? If anything, our criminal system is a plea bargain factory. Exact numbers are hard to find but one source we found claimed—on a federal level—criminal plea bargains rose ten percent from eighty-four percent in 1984 to ninety-four percent in 2001. Not a bad track record for something that only showed up in 1970.

The 'Lectric Law *Library* defines a plea bargain as*: A negotiated agreement between the defense and the prosecution in a criminal case. Typically the defendant agrees to plead guilty to a specified charge in exchange for an oral promise of a lower sentence.*

As we mentioned earlier, once an arrest is made the machine starts its process. One of the easier ways to understand this is the clock has started for the prosecution. They must come to a resolution as soon as possible. What's the hurry? The Sixth Amendment mandates your right to a speedy trial. They can't leave you rotting in a cell for years without a trial (a common tactic in merry ol' England back when the U.S. Constitution was written). Today the state wants to bring your case to a conclusion as *fast* and as *cheaply* as possible so it can move on to the next one.

Why do some cases drag on for years before going to trial? Usually the defense attorney stalls things. Officially it's so your team has ample time to prepare your best defense. In actual practice, however, things are a little more complex. Don't forget we are talking about a system that runs on money and metrics. Plea deals solve everyone's problems.

For the layperson this means your attorney and the prosecutor get together—for your guilty plea to a lesser charge—and the matter is put to bed. While you may not agree if you acted in actual self-defense understand that pleas are very popular with the typical players in the legal game.

- For criminals, they are a sweet deal. Instead of being punished for what they actually did they cop a plea and do less time.
- For the state, it saves the cost of a trial (and the chance of losing).
- For judges, it rubber stamps the case and gets it off their desk by sending it down the line to the correctional system.
- For the prosecutor, it counts as a conviction. A high conviction rate benefits his or her career.
- For the DA, it means re-election (their numbers now show how tough he or she is on crime).
- For your attorney, he or she is handsomely compensated for what amounts to a collective day's worth of reading and negotiating.

Then along you come with your claim of self-defense...

You may not want to take a plea deal if you were truly acting in self-defense because you feel you were in the right. How could you be convicted for being right? By rejecting a plea deal you throw a monkey wrench into the way things normally work. But also realize you're swimming upstream, and the water is poisoned. The system is biased toward pleas because they count as 'wins' in a metric-driven field. In fact when you look at the system it has very little reason to drop charges once an arrest is made. What's in it for them? They don't go to prison if you lose, and there's the issue of their precious conviction rate.

That brings up another tanker truck of toxic dumped in the stream. They'll throw the book at you for daring to fight. The official position is denial, but the system is like a schoolyard bully. They don't like it when people stand up to them so they get extra vicious if you do. If you don't take the plea you'd *better* win.

This is over and above how many defense attorneys will really push you to take a plea—even if it was actual self-defense. While they'll fight, *it is going to cost you.* The raw truth is given the amount of money most people have for their defense, their attorney is just a high-priced plea negotiator.

10. *To prosecute or not to take the plea or not.* Let's talk about added incentives. Or to be more exact perverse incentives. We've mentioned prosecutors use plea deals as a carrot-and-stick scenario. The carrot is less jail time for confessing to a lesser charge. The stick is they'll throw the book at you if you don't take it.

Does this sound hopeless? It's not. But you *do* have to know what you're up against (you're the wounded moose facing the three-headed bear). So let's talk about another invisible force when it comes to both plea bargains and being charged—economics. It plays a role in both.

If the state doesn't think it can make charges stick—barring political pressure—it will hold off until prosecutors believe they can. Often nothing happens with the case, but it's *not* closed. The case file either seems to hang in limbo or you feel you're under the sword of Damocles (waiting for the knock on the door). It's strange to say, but you can be the victim of your own success. The better you articulate things while making your statement, the better your chances are that there'll be no arrest, but the case is still open.[10]

In the event of an arrest and after the prosecutor puts a check in his 'win box' there are still many opportunities. Criminals agreeing to lesser charges reduce prison overcrowding, cost of housing inmates, and ease parole pressures. Plea bargains also open more sentencing options to your attorney. He can argue for probation, house arrest, community service, halfway houses, group homes, and deferred sentences. These too reduce the strain on the prison system. This makes them more attractive to all involved—especially if your actions weren't self-defense.

Before you take the plea, however, make sure you ask your attorney *what you lose long term* by pleading to a lesser charge. You need to make an informed decision about what you avoid and what you step into.

A plea deal won't look attractive if it was self-defense. Even if you think it's self-defense, but it wasn't—like our buddy Tyler. By the end of this book you'll understand not just how Tyler dropped the ball, but why it shattered it into a million pieces. As a bit of advice before you claim self-defense, make sure that it really was.

---

10. What you want is called a "no bill." This officially closes the case. But that's going to cost you extra money, time, and research.

This is why Marc says: *The first person you have to convince (it was self-defense) is your own attorney—before you make a statement.*

Tyler Stories, Two and Three

Our friend Tyler is back but in two different incidents. (In this book, Tyler's behavior and training change a lot. And if you ever are confused when we refer to a Tyler tale, we put them all in the back for quick reference

Tyler story, Two:

Tyler has spent years training in martial arts. He even learned some decent mixed martial arts (MMA) moves. He's been repeatedly told and believes he can defend himself. One night Brittany sends him to the market. Coming out of the store, he notices three dudes following him to his car. Confident he can handle himself, he keeps walking. They speed up, and one calls out to him. Tyler stops, turns to face them, and aggressively demands, What do you want?" Two spread out from the guy in the middle who asks Tyler for money to buy beer.

Tyler refuses and adds a few insults. The speaker angrily asks, "What's your problem?" Tyler drops his groceries and takes a fighting stance. There's a blinding flash in his head on the left, and a sharp pain in his right side. Collapsing to the ground, he's beaten and robbed. The muggers flee. Tyler gets up, staggers back into the store, and the ambulance is called.

He lives, but it takes months to recover from the stabbing and concussion. Tyler didn't bring a knife to a gunfight, he brought bare hands against a gang of armed robbers.

Tyler Story, Three:

Tyler is a concealed carry permit holder. In his training the term "self-defense" was thrown around a lot, but never clearly defined. Tyler's running errands before meeting Brittany. Due to a long supermarket line he is running late. So he drives a little fast in the parking lot. A smaller car pulls out from behind a bigger vehicle. Despite stomping the brakes and punching the horn in warning, Tyler hits the other car. A furious Tyler jumps out of his car. So does the other driver, a guy about Tyler's age. Tempers flare, words are exchanged about who's at fault, and both try to intimidate the other to back off. The other man shoves Tyler in the chest and tells him to get out of his face. Tyler draws his gun and shoots him.

When the police arrive, Tyler claims he acted in self-defense. He shot the guy because he was "in fear for his life." Tyler contends the guy was closing in to attack. Eye witnesses and video footage of the incident don't support that interpretation. In fact, they tell a completely different story.

Tyler is arrested for murder and ends up taking a manslaughter plea. This time, Tyler brought a gun to a fist fight.

In both these stories, Tyler reached limitations in his training he didn't know existed until it was too late.

When all you have is a hammer...

Training Limitations versus the Self-Defense Spectrum

When someone decides to learn self-defense, it can be confusing. And it's a scary subject. Much of what you're asked to do and learn is outside your comfort zone (emotionally and physically). The amount of information thrown at you can be overwhelming. You're not sure it's going to work. You mostly look for reassurance. While you have a vague sense of urgency often training is like doing a puzzle in the dark. The worst part about this is that without a bigger picture, it's difficult to tell when your instructor is giving you bad, incomplete, or spot-on advice. You don't know what you don't know. Add the appeal of 'you just do this' answers to sort out this complexity. All of this makes you vulnerable to soundbite SD. In time, you begin to make sense of what you're told. Since that's the purpose of communication, this understanding is pretty much a no-brainer.

But have you ever asked yourself what you're *not* being taught? Ask yourself if the information is *systematized or codified*. Those are terms we picked up from Liam Jackson. But we're mixing it with an explanation Marc got from Bob Orlando.

Combat techniques can be collected and put into a *system*. Typically combat systems are entirely focused on physical components. They are intentionally limited. Systems don't need to address other problems because they're taught inside—and as part of—a larger context (e.g., military or law enforcement). Systems work fine and dandy in those specific careers and environments. They can be hyper-focused on only the physical because:

- Related problems will be covered by *other* training.
- You'll be told when, where, and on whom to use these skills.
- Those giving you the orders have extra training and orders of their own.

Given those conditions, systems *don't have to be* all-encompassing.

Forget the macho. If you take a military combative or shooting system out of the original context and use them to teach civilians, you'll end up with students in trouble. Remember rules of engagement? Remember Jerome Ersland?[11] He was convicted of murder because he claimed he was following his military training. The problem with these systems isn't that they don't work; the trouble is they *do*. What systems don't teach is how to stay out of prison if you use what you're taught under civilian rules of engagement.

Codified systems *do* address other areas. For example, it is a rare martial art school that doesn't try to include character-building and ethical tenets (e.g., respect, courtesy, integrity, perseverance, self-control). As much as these are dismissed by adherents of combat systems, such tenets are at least an attempt to address mental preparation. (If for no other reason than to keep you out of unnecessary trouble.)

But how often do you hear in a martial arts school about handling the legal aftermath? While some shooting academies offer training in the legal aftermath, how much time is spent on the ethical and emotional problems of using lethal force on another human? ow much time is spent teaching you to recognize when it *isn't* time to shoot? These are just some of the differences and nuances of all the available types of training. Now you can clearly see how easily the four components can be missed or overshadowed by the more fun physical stuff.

Before we risk being burned at the stake let's address what we mean by training. We aren't talking about watching YouTube videos (that's something else). Training is scheduled, instructor-led classes. It's also you or your company paying a legitimate subject matter expert. A key point about how training differs from education, the class is focused on a specific topic. We'll stick to discussing martial arts and firearms training—even though well-rounded self-defense training encompasses much more.

Now back to us burned at the stake. Differences and divisions between martial arts and firearms training are not only dangerous, they're wrong. Dangerous because each 'camp' tries to define self-defense by its own tools and pretends the other facets

---

11. https://on.wsj.com/2s9RTFp

aren't important. That leaves you as the trainee unprepared for all the other ways violence and crime happen. Wrong because… that takes a little more explaining.

Commonly martial arts (MA) and firearms training are viewed as different camps, and each claim to have the 'right answers' about self-defense. This approach is wrong because they're *not* unique subjects. They are *different points on the same spectrum*.

The spectrum of defending yourself ranges from a polite no to going hands-on to killing someone. Either camp that claims to have 'all' the answers is like two fleas arguing over who owns the dog—and that argument does get heated. Without knowing it, you've probably been recruited into a particular flea's camp. Before we go down that road know this: Both camps have important information and teach skills necessary for a wide range of options that ensure your safety.

Here's where things get wobbly: All of your needs *won't* be solved with bare hands. *Nor* does every self-defense situation require deadly force. (The Tyler two and three stories show exactly that.) Violence varies so the same response *doesn't* work everywhere and every time. There' are also the life skills you need to learn to be assertive without becoming aggressive and the ability to emotionally control yourself in verbal conflicts. Kicking or shooting training won't address those.

Also, instructors won't stay in business long if they tell people all the things they're not teaching. Nor will they stay in business if they tell people self-defense includes more than the tools they teach. Instead instructors will offer more in-depth training on the one piece of the puzzle they know. For example, constant new katas in martial arts and low-light 'funhouse' shooting. Or if you've been around a while, there are the instructor 'certification' and recertification courses. (It's beyond the scope of this book, but, there are some serious problems with what is being taught about 'teaching' at certificate mills.) This is a monumental disservice to trainees that results in people trained in depth on very narrow topics, who then believe they're educated about a much wider subject.[12]

---

12. There are good teachers who can adequately introduce you to self-defense. These instructors have a wider and more complete curriculum designed to help you get where you need to go. If they can't teach you some SD facet, they enthusiastically refer you to another expert. The key is they think of self-defense *as a big picture* not a specialization.

Welcome to a conflict of interests. As an individual, *you* need to have options other than pulling the trigger or throwing a punch. (A good mix or at least an understanding of your training gives you more options for appropriate responses.) This almost puts you at odds with the needs of the instructor. It's in the instructor's financial interest to keep you attending and paying. That's one reason camps form in this business.

And there are more than just two camps. Within camps there are divisions, rifts, rivalries, and competition among schools. What we're about to say applies to the camps and schools. Each is vying for your business and in its general category *is selling the same basic product*. To attract attention, they *have* to present what they sell as 'superior.' This isn't just between the two major camps, it also includes subcamps. (What's the best martial art style for self-defense? What's the best caliber for self-defense?) Each claim to have not only the answer but superior knowledge. Often this emphasis on being better than the competition comes at the expense of ingraining working skills in and providing well-rounded knowledge to you, the student.

Not all the blame can be laid at the instructor's doorstep. These camps and schools rely on a fan base. Fandom exerts a subtle but real pressure to 'join the club.' There's also a sense of belonging that makes people feel good. They have special knowledge and shared activities to bond over. (A tribe if you will.) The deeper you go into one of the training camps it narrows your focus and the more you believe you address the bigger subject This happens in subtle ways you typically can't see if you don't know to look.

Students happily join these *one-stop shopping for all your self-defense needs* camps. Often they take as gospel whatever the instructor says about self-defense. Anybody who's spent time bouncing between schools knows how fanatical people can get about their guru, camp, and soundbites.

Fanaticism is often the result of entrenched 'knowledge.' We mentioned it earlier, but let's expand it. It's a bigger concept, but we're going to introduce it in terms of your 'first instructor.' Often information from someone's first instructor is cemented as what is 'right.' It doesn't matter what the information is, the student believes that's *how it's done*. (For example, how to throw a punch or hold a gun.) Once embedded it becomes the lens through which all other information is viewed, including rejection of any information different from what the person 'thinks' he knows. If a new instructor presents different information it's often met with blank stares, disapproval, or outright hostility because it reconciled with what the student has already filed under 'correct information' (even if the new information is more effective or safer). If you've been told, "Well, that's not what my last instructor told me..." you're hearing this in action.[13]

It's easy to see entrenched knowledge as 'first instructor syndrome.' What's harder to see is the repeating pattern—especially when it comes to self-defense's big picture. With a puzzle of so many pieces, you'll have many first ideas you never heard much less imagined. These often are framed as models. Models serve as guidelines for complex subjects (e.g., a threat assessment model [explaining how to spot danger]). The problem is the *first* model students are exposed to often becomes set in stone. Anything different or that doesn't fit that first model is ignored or argued against.

For example, the attitude of _____ (insert threat assessment model) is the right one. We give you multiple threat assessment models. It's not a matter of which one is *right*, it's which one works for *you*. If you didn't know there was more than one welcome to first instructor syndrome.

The big picture of self-defense requires you to move into numerous areas—each goes beyond your comfort zone. Part of the appeal of these camps is they become your new and improved comfort zone. It's comfortable to stay instead of branching out.

To add another level of complexity how current is your "I know that"? So what computer operating system did you learn first? What are you on now? How many changes between those two systems? The same applies to what you 'know' about self-defense. t doesn't hurt to go back and check if the information you have is still valid. What still works and what has changed? Now, how does this apply to training? The same effect can apply to what instructors know. How dated is the information they're providing?

We've introduced you to just a few of the unseen influences in self-defense training. Often the fixation *on training* becomes more important than what you're preparing for. It's easy to get so caught up in the details that you lose sight of what's is and isn't relevant to self-defense.

---

13. While it may be a legitimate struggle to reconcile information, it's rude to the instructor (because students not seeking something new are trying to validate what they think they already know). It's also disruptive for the rest of the class.

We want you to keep this in mind as you read the rest of this book. Unfortunately much of what is being called self-defense training has mutated into business and camps. As long as you never need to 'use your training' these practices are sustainable and won't really hurt you. But, if you are ever in a situation where you need to use your training you need skills that work outside the self-defense equivalent of academia.

You keep on using that word
I do not think it means
what you think it means.
Princess Bride

Legal Argle-Bargle

Ready for another major paradigm shift? Think about self-defense less as *what you do* and more about *what you don't do.* This perspective change will do more to reveal what you weren't taught about self-defense than any amount of lecturing about what's wrong with most training. Everyone's so focused on doing they don't pay attention to:

1. When not to do. This goes beyond shoot and no shoot decisions and into other considerations—including do you have to engage? Can the situation be better resolved if you turn and walk away? (Tyler, Three)

2. What not to do. Another complex issue but for brevity's sake we'll just ask: Does the situation require more force than you brought with you? It's not what people in self-defense training want to hear, but it can be better to let yourself be safely robbed than try to use insufficient force (Tyler, Two)

3. Know when to stop. This is easily understood as when you keep acting after the threat passed. This is where most people cross out of the limits of self-defense and into excessive force and imperfect self-defense. (Look up that term.)

4. Excessive force. To keep it short the example we'll give is you using a strike enhancer in what was an empty hand situation. You may win but you've also bumped the charges you face to 'aggravated ____ (whatever they call it in your state). (Both Tyler One and Three.)

Keep Tyler and those four points in mind as you read the rest of this chapter.

Too often people look up their state self-defense laws then claim they know their right to use self-defense. Yeeeeeah, about that...

First, these future jailhouse lawyers do *not* look up other laws regarding violence. When you do you'll find *all kinds* of limits, qualifiers, and "If you ____ it's illegal" restrictions. In fact if you look those restrictions show up *in* the self-defense statute. We live in Colorado, so we're going to use what's local to explain this idea. (Go look up your own state statutes):

> CO Revised Statutes 18-1-704 Use of Physical Force in Defense of a Person
>
> •(Part 1) Use of Physical Force in defense of a person(1) Except as provided in subsections (2) and (3) of this section, a person is justified in using physical force upon another person in order to defend himself or a third person from what he reasonably believes to be the use or imminent use of unlawful physical force by that other person, and he may use a degree of force which he reasonably believes to be necessary for that purpose.
>
> (2) Deadly physical force may be used only if a person reasonably believes a lesser degree of force is inadequate…

Not exactly the free pass many people in training want to believe it is. Here are even more restrictions from the same statute:

(3) Notwithstanding the provisions of subsection (1) of this section, a person is not justified in using physical force if:

(a) With intent to cause bodily injury or death to another person, he provokes the use of unlawful physical force by that other person; or

(b) He is the initial aggressor; except that his use of physical force upon another person under the circumstances is justifiable if he withdraws from the encounter and effectively communicates to the other person his intent to do so, but the latter nevertheless continues or threatens the use of unlawful physical force; or

(c) The physical force involved is the product of a combat by agreement not specifically authorized by law.

If that isn't bad enough let's look at the Colorado law regarding fighting:

§ 18-13-104. Fighting by agreement - dueling

(1) If two or more persons shall fight by agreement in a public place, except in a sporting event authorized by law, the persons so fighting commit a class 1 petty offense.

(2) Persons who by agreement engage in a fight with deadly weapons, whether in a public or private place, commit dueling, which is a class 4 felony.

Notice a running theme regarding *both* your participation in the creation and escalation of an incident? Self-defense is not fighting or mutual combat or consensual or whatever they call it in your state. Most people can't imagine doing violence to another person except under emotional extremes, and *most* violence is an extension of conflict. The cops will look for your participation, and that's what the prosecutor will try to sell to the jury. A very good summation is: Self-defense is when you have no other good option. Fighting is when you're part of the problem. If the cop decides and the prosecutor can sell that you were involved *in the creation of circumstances that led to violence,* you're screwed—especially if they're right.

Are you beginning to understand why what you do *before* physical violence is so important to what happens afterward? Are you also catching on to why if you fight you don't want to try to claim self-defense? If the judge—after reviewing the evidence—*doesn't* allow you to claim self-defense in court, you've confessed to your crime. (¿Como se de se, "Plea deal time"?)

If you're going to pretend to be a legal eagle and know the law about your right to self-defense, you'd better stay within the parameters of self-defense. Lawyers deal with a lot of 'bad' self-defense claims that can be completely bogus (e.g., drug deals gone bad and fights) but more often are bad because someone did something that invalidates the self-defense defense. As many cases as a defense attorney sees, the cops and courts see even more. They have lots of experience gutting such claims and that also applies to you—even if you truly acted in self-defense.

Before you think you understand self-defense law take a class. (If for no other reason than to learn the difference between statutory and case law.) Spend time to look up the other laws regarding violence. Otherwise you'll be trying to claim self-defense when you armed yourself, left your house, went down the road to pursue a disagreement, and shot someone in what you were sure was 'self-defense' (Tyler in Story One and Raul Rodriguez—the guy serving life for murder).

Second—and why we called this chapter "Legal Argle-Bargle"— 'knowing' the law isn't enough. One of the absolutely worst things you can say about self-defense training is, "I know that already." We're talking about a complex, multi-variant topic. Odds are there are many levels deeper than what you know. An example is when we say 'knowing the law' isn't enough, it starts in an incredibly basic place.

What words mean.

In a legal context, common words mean something completely different than the way lay people use them. We're not just talking different, but very specific definitions. For example, the Colorado statute reads "... a person is justified in…" What does that word "justified" mean to you?

Take the time to think about what it meant to you before you started reading.

Once again going to the 'Lectric Law Library their definition of justification is: *The act by which a party accused shows and maintains a good and legal reason in court, why he did the thing he is called upon to answer.*

Built into the legal definition of *justification* is 'explaining' your actions. It's not just saying you were justified, it's proving it! Remember that line in the Colorado statute "...a person is justified in using physical force ..." How many think that's permission for whatever they want to call self-defense? Before you picked this book up did you?

There are other ideas you need to look into before you tell yourself what you are about to do is self-defense. Things aren't as carte blanche as many people think they are. You'll see that after Googling these terms:

- Self-defense defense
- Immediate/imminent threat
- Lawful and unlawful use of force
- Imperfect self-defense
- Grievous or serious bodily injury
- Robbery and theft (big difference)
- Murder
- Manslaughter
- Brandishing and menacing
- Assault
- Battery
- Aggravated assault (or whatever it's called in your state)
- Aggravated murder
- Maiming
- Weapon dangerous or deadly
- Lethal force instrument
- Duty
- Duty to retreat
- Stand your ground
- Castle Doctrine
- Trespass
- Property rights
- Responsibility
- Disparity of force (this isn't a legal term, but it's important for you to understand)

Once you have looked into these and how they apply in your state, you'll need to sit down and reconsider what you've been told—especially about using weapons (improvised or de facto) on your fellow citizens.

One more thing—that second to last one—responsibility. It's kind of a big one. In this book you'll occasionally see the phrase "participation in the creation and escalation of a situation." This is where most people fall down when it comes to self-defense. Responsibility is kind of like icy concrete steps. Your attorney tries to give you a handrail, opposing counsel wants to shove you. The prosecutor tries to assign responsibility by giving your actions the worst interpretation possible—regardless of what you meant to do. This will be easy if your actions actually did set up the circumstances that resulted in violence (e.g., Tyler One and Three). During the pre-violence and violence stages of the incident, it's *really* easy to do something that will send you tumbling down the icy steps in the aftermath. This is why it's really important to get control of your ego, take extra care with your actions before violence, and to try to avoid it whenever possible.

Actions and responsibility are areas where the law doesn't gel well with human psychology—especially when we're adrenalized and scared. The law doesn't care what you *meant*. . . (That only really matters to you—and Tyler, One.) We cannot stress enough that the prosecutor will sell the worst possible interpretation of your actions. If you said or did anything to help that sale, you will be hit over the head with it.

For example, someone is in your face and you feel threatened. You may snarl something, hoping to scare him off (to avoid violence). That's a *very* common human strategy and motivation. But the DA will spin it as you provoking and escalating a verbal disagreement to a physical fight. It doesn't stop at just words. Using poor old Tyler in story one the prosecutor sells it as he armed himself before he went down the street to pick a fight. (Or in real life Raul Rodriguez.)

Watch for both police and prosecutors trying to assign responsibility to you.

Tyler Story, Four

It's Christmas Eve. Tyler and Brittany are at the home of her divorced mom. But there's a potential hitch because Tyler and Brittany's brother Braden have an antagonistic history. Braden, a roofer, has had a bad break-up and is staying with Mom until he gets back on his feet. Fortunately Braden is at dad's so everyone is in high spirits and having a good time. Then Braden walks in. It's clear he and dad were into the eggnog. He's back home because he and dad got into an argument.

Braden starts drinking again and begins to hurl insults. Tyler initially tells him to calm down. For the sake of the family, he suggests a truce even if it is just for the evening. This pisses off Braden, and he swings at Tyler, who quickly backs away. Braden tries to hit him again, and Tyler punches him. Braden charges and tackles Tyler. Landing badly, Tyler hits his head and is momentarily stunned. In his drunken rage, Braden kneels on top of Tyler and starts to strangle him. The women try to pull him off, but he's too strong. His air cut off, Tyler goes into survival mode, pulls his pocket knife, and stabs Braden. The knife misses Braden's arm and goes into his chest. The paramedics are called, but Braden dies en route to the hospital.

Tyler tries to explain that he panicked because he couldn't breathe. It's the best description he can find, but the word panic doesn't go over well. Tyler was correct in recognizing his life was in danger but couldn't explain why the circumstances were life-threatening. Instead it sounds like he freaked out. The investigating officer keeps referring to the entire incident as a "fight." Tyler doesn't correct him.

What Tyler doesn't know is that the DA has been told in a phone call an edited version of events and has ordered Tyler arrested. From that moment on, all the questions Tyler is asked by the police are aimed at building the state's case and undermining his claim of self-defense.

Tyler is charged with murder one. Sure that he acted in self-defense, Tyler refuses to take a plea. Given the history between Tyler and Braden, the prosecution argues premeditation. The state continually refers to the incident as a fight and argues that lethal force was not justified. Tyler was unable to articulate that being choked while on the ground was different from fighting and rolling around. He is convicted and sent to prison.

Author's note: This story is the perfect storm. Remember mental gear shifts? The ones about it depends being the right answer and high speed problem-solving. If any one of the variables change so does the outcome. Examples are: If Braden had never come home; if there hadn't been alcohol involved; if Braden hadn't choked Tyler; if Tyler stabbed Braden in a different spot... On and on it goes. It's also why being able to convey pre-existing knowledge, objective circumstances and assessment are critical.

The difference between
theory and practice is—
in theory—there is no difference.

Threat Models, Information Sources, and the Map *Isn't* the Territory

You're about to read the longest chapter in this book. Be warned we intend for you to question your training paradigms and assumptions. This will ruffle some feathers, but these are things you really need to consider before using your training —especially if what you learned works to hurt people. (In fact, the more effective it is at injuring others, the more you need to consider your actions.) Think of this as the "anti blow-out" chapter. We're going to show you how to check your tires.

In Greek mythology, Cerberus was the three-headed dog that guarded the gates of Hades. The three topics we will discuss are like different heads that come from the same body. All of them are about the information gained in training, its relevance to your circumstances, and you actually using it. Any one of them can bite you.

This chapter may seem unrelated to the fourth Tyler story, but it lays the foundation for understanding why he (who acted in self-defense) was arrested and convicted.

Threat Models

What threat assessment model do you use?

If either 'what' or 'threat assessment model' make you say, "Huh?" You don't have a hole in your training, you have a Grand Canyon-sized abyss. Remember Liam Jackson's story about the prosecutor and blank looks (when asked why the defendant was in fear for his life)? Threat models are the first step to keep from being convicted because you can't answer the *why* question.

There are several court-tested threat models. The importance of 'court-tested' is that when you frame your responses within them:

- You get them into your statement.
- This introduces them into evidence that cannot be later rejected or denied.
- You demonstrate a pre-existing knowledge about danger.
- You indicate training in the subject.
- You communicate to the investigating officer in terms he not only understands but would use to justify his own professional use of force.
- Unless you've seriously screwed up in other ways it makes it more difficult to prosecute you for defending yourself. (Remember metrics and money?)
- You've pre-empted the prosecutor's *why* question. Your attorney can call in expert witnesses to confirm the standards you used were legitimate.
- An expert can further explain to the jury why your perception of danger was reasonable given the circumstances.
- An expert can expand (and do damage control) on things you couldn't explain well.

Each of those points is worth entire volumes. For brevity's sake we won't go into details,[14] but the second bullet point bears further consideration. Especially with higher levels of force, *it's critical* you are videoed making your statement and having your attorney present. We won't go into the whys, but this pre-existing knowledge *must* be embedded in your statement.

Now that we've tipped you off about how important a threat assessment model is let's contradict ourselves. It *doesn't* matter which one you use—it does matter that you have one.

That's because threat assessment is not set in concrete. At best these models are systematized attempts to create a framework to describe a complex problem. If that's too academic for you try this: *They are ways to recognize and later explain dangerous circumstances in a consistent, and understandable manner.* That's

---

14. Remember this book is an introduction. The subject of threat assessment is very complex. Professionals in the field continue to argue interpretation and application. Since they all have valid points, it's worth your time to listen to these 'debates.'

crucial when it comes to keeping your brains from being blown into a fine pink mist, as well as, answering questions from people unhappy with your use-of-force decision.

The grandfather of all modern threat assessment models is AOI (ability opportunity, and intent). AOI arose from police-involved shootings. To understand its significance (and all other models) you have to know that in U.S. criminal law the prosecution must "prove beyond a reasonable doubt" the *means, motive,* and *opportunity* to do the crime. That translates into proving the criminal had the ability to act (how it was done, means), intent (why), and the chance to act (opportunity).

By basically lining out the *same* factors necessary for a criminal conviction from the other side—AOI gave an officer a way to explain why shooting was a reasonable response to a situation. (As a side note: Despite squeals from certain individuals that police get away with murdering people in the streets, the ability to articulate the situation in these terms is why so many officer-involved shootings are cleared in the officer's favor.) Prosecutors can't bitch when the same standards they exploit to convict are used to exonerate people. Well they can, but tough noogies.

After grandpa **a**bility, **o**pportunity, **i**ntent (AOI) there are other common threat assessment models:

- **A**bility, **o**pportunity, **j**eopardy (AOJ)
- **J**eopardy, **a**bility, **m**eans (JAM)
- **I**ntent, **m**eans, **o**pportunity, **p**reclusion (IMOP)
- **A**bility, **o**pportunity, **j**eopardy, **p**reclusion (AOJP)
- The Five Stages

A few points: Jeopardy is commonly used to replace intent because of the contention by prosecutors that "you aren't a mind reader" and can't tell someone's intent. (Stop and savor the hypocrisy of this for a moment.) Means and opportunity are interchangeable. The addition of P (preclusion) isn't exclusive to AOJ; it can be added to any of the models that are based on legal tactics.

Some down and dirty definitions starting with the AOJ model:

Ability: Your opponent has the power to attack, kill, or cripple (weapon or physical ability—including disparity of force).

Opportunity or Means: The attacker or potential assailant is able to able to immediately employ *that ability*. While the concept is consistent, the manifestation depends on circumstances. For example, the person's ability (empty hand versus knife versus club versus gun) changes the range or distance he has to cover to successfully attack you. Someone with empty hands across the street does *not* have the opportunity or means to attack you (unless he crosses the street). Someone with a gun *does*—unless you're behind a brick wall, looking out a bullet-proof glass window. See how opportunity or means change according to circumstances? (We also recommend you look into the difference between cover and concealment when it comes to gunfire.)

Another important consideration in opportunity and means is obstacles. Is there nothing but air between you? Or is there a physical barrier that prevents or hinders his attack? For example, a long table he'd have to run around (or over) to reach you. Know this: Who comes around that table has a lot to do with a successful claim of SD. But someone—lacking a gun—who tries to close the distance (to use what they have) is a good articulation point that you can use to explain how the person attempted *to develop* opportunity or the means to attack you.

Jeopardy: If the elements of ability, opportunity, and means are present, you must also be able to explain to the cops, attorneys, or the jury why the level of force you used was reasonable in that situation. In the case of lethal force self-defense, it is *when the opponent is acting in such a way that a reasonable and prudent person would conclude the attacker intended to kill or cripple.* (Marty Hayes) Another way jeopardy is commonly understood is when the person acts in a manner consistent with what it takes to commit a crime or attack someone. You can explain he set you up for a robbery in terms of jeopardy. As we said earlier, jeopardy *can* replace intent because it can't be attacked as 'mind reading.' (It will be attacked in other ways.)

Intent: (in legal terms) *The determination or resolve to do a certain thing, or the state of mind with which something is done.*[15] This can get you accused of being a mind reader, but there are reasons it's still used. Marc uses a slightly modified version: *When a person crosses a mental boundary that gives self-permission for violence and the human body prepares for physical violence* (adrenaline and involuntary physiological reactions). That's to say there are identifiable changes in the body language of someone about to commit violence as well as physiological indications—like skin color, pupil size, and unconscious muscle tension. So you

15. https://bit.ly/2ICfVzE

can—literally—see when someone intends to attack you. (If you're good, you can see when he makes the decision to attack.)

The question is: *Can you articulate what you saw?*

> Important safety tip: Preclusion is the Achilles' heel of many legitimate self-defense claims—especially in states that have a duty to retreat law. If you can explain why there was no other safe option that's a big shield for your defense. Learning about preclusion is another homework assignment if you don't like prison showers.

Preclusion: Could you have done anything other than use force to ensure your safety? Putting it another way: could you have done something to remove yourself from the situation or did you have no other choice than to use force? Before you try to answer that question, your answer should be based on the following factors: the time you had available, exits, terrain, their numbers, and positions.

Before we move to the Five Stages, we will throw in another phrase relevant to all these models. That is "totality of the circumstances." The following explanation is legal argle-bargle, but it has to be that way. *The totality of the circumstances suggests that there is no single factor to base a use-of-force decision on. You must take into consideration all the facts and context to conclude from the whole picture that you acted appropriately* (Massad Ayoob).

Totality of circumstances is the best armor against the prosecution's main attack strategy. When you say you saw something and it meant ___, the prosecutor will nitpick. That's where totality of circumstances comes in. As an analogy, think about a brick. By itself, a single brick doesn't mean much, and it *could* be used in many different ways. The prosecutor will ask, "Is it possible that brick could be used as a paperweight?" The answer *has* to be yes because it is possible—not probable but possible. However, when bricks are put together *in a certain way*, they form a wall. In the context of a wall, a particular brick's significance is a matter of high probability—not endless possibilities. It's part of a wall, not a paperweight.

Again, it doesn't matter what threat assessment model you use. The elements of that model are the wall (the totality of circumstances). The details *of the incident* are the different bricks. When you see a specific brick *in this context*, it means only one thing. With a threat assessment model you can explain that.

Five Stages of Violent Crime: In some ways this is a stand-alone model from the previous alphabet soups. In another way it's exactly what you need to describe them—especially jeopardy. The five are stages all violent crimes go through to achieve their goal. From there it's just a matter of style, speed, and sequence. More than that the five teach crime avoidance because once you know the process you can try to derail it before it reaches physical violence (stage four). The five are:

- Intent
- Interview
- Position
- Attack
- Reaction

Intent you already know. Interview is how the criminal determines if you're safe to attack (his safety check). Positioning is him (or them) putting himself into location or position to successfully attack. Attack is the physical assault *or* threat of overwhelming force (e.g., pulling a gun to rob you). Reaction is the criminal's emotional response to what he did.

As for crime avoidance, if the criminal cannot develop the first three stages, the attack *won't* occur (his plans will be derailed). You have the ability to derail his plans without using physical force. If he attempts to force the attack[16] that provides a justifiable reason for your decision and action.

Here's the real value of the five: if you don't see these developing, *there is no danger.*[17] So take a chill pill.

Another advantage of threat assessment models is they give you terms to describe dangerous circumstances. There is industry jargon that's widely known and understood by subject matter experts in a given field. For example, *disparity of force* can mean these elements are present: weapon versus bare hands, size, disparity of numbers, able-bodied versus handicapped, man versus woman, and positional disadvantage. (Tyler was at a positional disadvantage, impeded by being stunned, and choked by a stronger attacker while pinned on the ground and unable to escape. Was there an immediate threat of death or grievous bodily injury?

---

16. Amateur versus professional: An older more professional criminal will just move on to another ATM as a robbery site. Younger, more squirrely ones will try to force the issue.

17. In case you're wondering what happened to the fifth stage, it's more for threat assessment professionals. It's whether the person will use this strategy again.

Arguably so. Unfortunately he didn't know how to explain it.) You don't have to be perfect, but you do have to know enough to get the idea into your statement. Even if you're not a whiz-bang expert who can fully explain these terms there are professionals *who can*.

Again, it doesn't matter what model you use. What matters is you *have* one. A threat assessment model helps you:

- avoid an incident
- mentally prepare for action
- assess how much force you'll need
- keep from being arrested
- in court if you are arrested

Kinda useful don't you think?

Information Sources

It is critical you get information *relevant* to your circumstances and self-defense needs. That simple statement has some big implications. Two of which are:

1. This section has a lot to do with keeping you out of prison showers.

2. There are instructors to whom what we say *doesn't* apply.[18]

But numbers lie with instructors where it is valid but who tell themselves they've addressed 'this problem.' There are still other programs that glorify in 'previous experience' and use it as a marketing tool. (After this section, you'll know how to spot the difference.)

In the self-defense industry—but especially in firearms training—there is a *consumer* bias to have instructors who are or were LEOs or in the military. Many people believe that knowledge of one field is applicable to others so these instructors are the best. It's great that consumers want to get the finest training available, but there can be a slight hitch.

For example, an instructor with a military or law enforcement background can teach you how to shoot (a shooting system). But that's not where there are potential problems. These lie in the nonphysical—specifically information about when to pull the trigger.

---

18. We know and have studied with many of them. The caveat is that their information is practical for civilian use. This is because they worked to vet information by running it past experts in other fields. Just like we did for this book.

Unless trainers have consciously groomed their information *for civilian application,* there will be many unconscious biases and assumptions from their old professions and training. It was important for them to know things in 'that unique way' in their jobs' context. This framework affects everything. How they think, organize, reference, understand, talk about, and teach this information.

Three points can help you understand how this can influence your training and why it can be a problem:

One is the difference between military, law enforcement, and civilian resources, duties, and jobs.

Civilians don't have close air support, artillery, drone-guided missiles, or heavily armed squads around them while in a hostile country. You don't have the radio back-up, legal authority, training, or bullet-proof vests police have.

That's okay because you also don't do their jobs. You probably won't be shot at like police or military personnel. You *don't* have to gear up and hunt dangerous people who want to shoot or blow you up. This may sound silly when we put it this way, but we cannot stress enough how different resources and jobs influence thinking in countless ways. Starting with you—as a civilian—*don't* have a *duty to act*. You won't be sued or court-martialed for not engaging. You can run fiercely (in fact, if possible, we highly recommend doing so).

Despite the credibility we grant someone with military or law enforcement experience if an instructor doesn't *consciously* learn about the civilian parameters, he'll often subconsciously continue to think along previous lines. We'll give you an example in a minute. Often the information he provides is more applicable to his old circumstances (e.g., military, shoot to kill) and less to the ones you'll find yourself in (e.g., civilian, shoot to stop a threat).

If you want extra benefits from learning from a cop ask him what *his* goals were when questioning suspects. And you might want to ask what you should do when officers first arrive on scene. For example: Drop the gun means *drop the gun* not gingerly set it on the ground. (This is one of those 'you won't know about until it happens' problems we mentioned.) There's ingrained resistance to dropping the gun, because of safety and expense. You might hesitate when the order is given and get shot. "Drop it" is a time-sensitive issue.

Two is different rules of engagement.

Rules of engagement (ROE) for the military are completely different than civilian rules. Military ROE have nothing to do with common law or this country's legal system. Law enforcement also has a *duty to act*. Going back to legal argle-bargle, 'duty' is a legal obligation that you can be punished (fines, judgment, or prison) if you don't act. You *don't* have a duty to act. That gives you more options and exposes you to prosecution if you don't take them.

Remember that promised example? Jenna shows her students security camera crime footage so they can think how they might act in the same situation. On a number of occasions, there have been former LEO's in the room. The overwhelming response from cops, when asked what they would have done, is "I woulda chased him." That's a great LEO response, but not so much for a civilian.

Do you see how an instructor with a law enforcement background might affect your training? Starting with he may not know he has to squish the common 'if I have a gun I can act like a cop' mentality. He may not realize he has to *actually* tell you that if you 'give chase' you've stepped outside of self-defense. (You will be prosecuted for the shoot-out—especially if you win.) It's such a no-brainer to him, it's easy to forget it's news to everyone else.

What about military training and ROEs? A downed infantry opponent is still a combatant. (Down doesn't mean he can't shoot you.) Pass a living, but wounded combatant and that person becomes a prisoner. As a prisoner, you must render aid to him. So what do you do? In combat, you shoot him again *before* you pass him. It's a smart and safe battlefield tactic. In a civilian context, it's murder (or depending on your state, manslaughter).

An example Jenna used in her book *Calling the Shots* is Oklahoma City pharmacist Jerome Ersland. Two robbers entered the store and ordered employees to hand over drugs and money. The robbers fired shots, Ersland pulled a semi-automatic pistol from his pants pocket, fired, and the bullet struck one of the robbers in the head. The robber fell to the floor, then Ersland chased the second robber *from the store*. When Ersland returned to the store, he retrieved a second gun from a nearby drawer and fired five more shots into the chest of the unconscious robber. In his defense, Ersland claimed he acted according to his military training. He was convicted of first-degree murder because the second round of shots was characterized as a separate event from the first shot that incapacitated the robber. Even if we allow for 'military training,' he passed a downed combatant *twice* before executing him.

Another example: Marc has a story about a commercial martial arts school where he witnessed the owner teaching a neck break from behind—on a downed opponent. (That's a sentry removal technique.) The black belts diligently watched what their 'shihan' showed them. Seeing Marc's horrified expression the instructor quickly added, "this move is only for self-defense," which just dug him in deeper. Civilian rules of engagement limit when you can snap someone's neck—especially from behind.

Three is assumed knowledge by both the student and instructor.

There's a lot of ego involved in what we will talk about here. But let's start with assumed knowledge, which is a mix of knowledge, physical skills, and 'big picture' understanding. Why is this an issue? Because most self-defense training is patchwork. To further muddy the waters, technical skills that are part of something else (like shooting or martial arts) are called 'self-defense training.' Self-defense training needs an actual context to exist. Physical skills alone do *not* self-defense make. (Just ask Tyler one, two, and three.) This results in an inconsistent collection of knowledge and physical skills. That becomes a problem when all you *do* know keeps you from seeing what you *don't* know.

This is where ego gets in the way. As instructors, we often see students who don't t want to take a training program's primary courses. They think their knowledge and skills are well beyond the 'beginner level.'

If you can remove yourself from what you think you already know and take a step back to learn it over again, there is a high probability you will see this information in a different light. This enables you to have a more useful application of the skill in question.

A shooting example: Jenna and Jeff's Level One range training teaches the fundamentals of shooting. Folks who "have been shooting" all their lives are not excited to go back to 'basics.' They often are insulted by the idea of returning to the fundamentals. It is worth noting that *every time* one of these Doubting Thomas types takes the class he or she learns something new and improves basic skills. (For example, the mechanics of trigger pull.)

A hands-on example: Marc often encounters advanced arts practitioners who can't punch through a wet Kleenex—and that's against a stationary target. They have the belt, but they weren't taught effective mechanics.

Here's something we've danced around but haven't come out and said it yet. Going back to the fundamentals can also get you out of holes you've dug yourself into and fix bad habits you've developed along the way.

There are several manifestations of assumed knowledge specific to students. One is the student who assumes the instructor is passing on *all* the information relevant to his or her needs. The assumption is the curriculum provides everything they need to know about 'self-defense.' (Put a push pin in this, we'll come back to it.)

A bigger problem is how often students assume an introduction to a topic is all they need. Taking a soundbite from an expert is often interpreted as knowing what's most important—and by extension all that you need to understand the subject. (This is the appeal of soundbites.) This book is a primer, but the concepts it introduces go far deeper than what is covered in a class or a seminar. Besides practice, there comes further research. You must have as much information as possible to truly understand an idea.

Here's the elephant in the room. What does self-defense mean to you? Marc's contract attorney has a saying: *Everyone knows what something means until there's a problem*. Boy howdy do we have a problem. Before you picked up this book what did self-defense mean to you? Odds are, you sought training that supported *your personal definition* not what self-defense really is. This bias makes spotting what is missing from training difficult. It's further compounded by the instructor telling you what he teaches is "self-defense." This no matter what it is or what he doesn't cover.

Returning to the physical, often students go through specific training. Training while important to a certain level of self-defense does not apply to a broader understanding of the subject. For example:

- How important is trigger pull to shooting?
- How important is it to using a handgun in self-defense?
- How important is it to handling Drunken Uncle Albert who took a swing at you when you tried to get him out the door at the family reunion?
- Does your training cover the full spectrum that is SD?

That spectrum you now know constitutes self-defense—including the ability to scale your use of force to any specific incident. Until now did you even know you needed it?

On the nonphysical side...well... we won't bother addressing that. By picking up this book, you've started to understand many problems about what you thought you knew. (Congratulations—that's a bold step.)

What about the assumption of knowledge on the instructor's side? Again, there are multiple manifestations.

The instructor often assumes the student already has a base of knowledge to build on. This may sound strange to you if you're a martial artist, but it really applies to other areas of self-defense training. Martial arts tend to be ongoing lessons that build and develop over time. Most self-defense training is typically one-and-done. (Example: People take a shooting class instead of gun lessons.) In both shooting and martial arts seminars, instructors will jump in and teach techniques assuming students have pre-existing skills and knowledge.

In the shooting world—because mistakes can be lethal on the range—big name instructors often will have assistant teaching staff. In the more advanced classes, these assistants keep their eyes on students or even bring those with sub-par skills up to speed so they can still get some benefit from the class. In some cases this means taking a student to a different area of the range and having a sidebar conversation or even instruction on a particular skill. This helps bring students who are falling behind in sync with the rest of the class. This one-on-one can enhance learning and make a stressful situation positive.

The financial angle... Let's flop this dead fish on the table. Some instructors lie for financial gain. They will overpromise and underdeliver. They'll claim something is self-defense when it isn't. They'll offer one-stop shopping for all your needs (Look at a martial arts school window and see how many styles are taught, as well as, self-defense.) They'll sell you what you want not what you need—all the while calling it self-defense. They'll pad the information to keep you as a student (learning never-ending streams of drills, katas, and techniques) for rank advancement. The other side of that coin is they'll promise you high ranking in a ridiculously short amount of time for an exorbitant amount of money. The list goes on and on. Such schools are all about making money to keep the doors open. When you look at this training from a financial angle, you'll see that this isn't about being able to better defend yourself. Often it's overemphasizing one aspect of what should be a wide knowledge base about the subject to keep you paying.

Gaps in your training get buried under a constant barrage of details so you lose sight of the flaws. Remember the bullet-proof vest analogy? This is how it happens. Instructors pass on the gaps in their knowledge to their students. The problems you face with holes in what you learn have been happening for a long time. Many instructors have those same holes in *their* training. They pass this incomplete information on to you.

The Map Is Not the Territory.

Violence is foreign territory for most people. Mental maps are important. To find your way through a situation you first have to know which *way to go.* (This includes what you're likely to encounter, what works to stop it, what doesn't, and what you must be prepared to do.[19]) Otherwise you're sitting in the middle of an infinity of options with limited time to choose an effective direction. We introduced you to threat assessment models so it's time to discuss the importance of knowing some of the many other models (or maps) regarding violence. Again, the one you choose is less important than having one.

Understand that no model, no map, no training is going to work if you don't pay attention to your surroundings. Whether you call them models or maps, you need *recognition, time,* and *distance* to apply them. An analogy would be driving. Slamming on the brakes isn't going to help when you're going 70 miles per hour and don't see the road hazard until it's twenty feet away. You didn't see it because you were texting (that's the paying attention part). Once his attack is launched, it's too late to start thinking in terms of threat models, maps, and avoiding danger. You need to start applying this knowledge and awareness long before things get to that point. The good news is we're going to help you do that—with an important caveat. It doesn't have to be an exhausting level of "awareness." It *does* have to be enough for you to recognize when something is out

---

19. Jenna struggles with being squeamish with certain training maps. She says: Without a gun the only chance I have is to bring a larger attacker to my level by disabling him (think eyes, fishhook, or tearing out his groin). I have to wrap my brain around sticking my fingers in another human's eyes, mouth, or going for the groin. This is a shock for me. The time to address that squeamishness is in training. Can I do it in real life? Yep. But only because I have maps for when, where and how. That puts useful tools in my toolbox. Not my first choice, but I will go there if I have no other options. Without these maps I'm lost.

of place *before* danger becomes unavoidable. The level of awareness we're talking about is the same as you not texting while driving.

The first question you need to ask isn't about the quality of the map (that someone tries to sell you). The question is: *Does it apply to your needs?* The philosophy and code of honor of samurai from 17th century Japan don't have much to do with your life in your current culture. Military buzzwords are 'tactikool', but they aren't useful when you make a run to the grocery store. You need maps that can get you where you need to go *now.*

Whatever mental maps or models you pick *have* to work with your lifestyle, needs, and the realities and limits you function within (just like professional models work for professionals' needs). Applicability to your circumstances is your litmus test *not* how effective an idea is for people with radios, helicopters, numbers, and armored vehicles. Yes shooters, we're talking to you. For martial artists, do you really think a dueling system from an honor culture where everyone has blades and corrupt (or absent) police enforcement is appropriate for the suburbs? Those are problems you'll face when your training is *too effective* for your circumstances.

The next comes in two related parts: First, what are the limits of the map? Second, what extra training do you need to apply it 'on the ground?'

Limits are more than what the map doesn't cover. They can pop up in some really weird ways. Take for example a spectrum or a wheel. One map (model) is that violence is a spectrum and different responses are appropriate for different levels. This linear model shows how an incident progresses through identifiable stages. Failure of a response to end the situation justifies moving your reaction up a level. Sound reasonable? Actually this is a great way to teach the idea of scaling force to *beginners*. In practice it can leave you bleeding on the ground. Another limit is the way a slick lawyer will demand to know why you didn't follow the model and try every step in the process before you resorted to physical force.

The other model is a wheel with a hub (you) in the middle. The wheel bends the linear spectrum into a circle. This isn't a teaching model—it's far more prescriptive. Within a wheel you assess the situation and react with appropriate force without wasting time with ineffective levels (and risking injury). Nor do you react with excessive force for the circumstances. The situation dictates what level of force you use. The wheel is more advanced and *far* more useful for application—especially for professionals. (Who don't know what kind of situation they'll walk into or will land in their laps out of nowhere). Even though it's more effective, *you can't start* with the wheel. It requires a lot more training, awareness, and experience (possibly years) to use it effectively in violent situations.

That brings us to the second part 'what extra training? We mentioned systems' limits, but this goes beyond that. What does it take to fully understand the concept? What does it take before you can act on it? By 'what does it take...' we're not talking about intestinal fortitude, but extra skill sets, knowledge, understanding, and abilities. If you don't have those you're just parroting a soundbite.

There are many popular models in self-defense training without much understanding attached to them (e.g., situational awareness, color codes, OODA loop). These 'terms' come from specific professions and if you are employed in those professions, you get the extra training that supports these models. That extra training is lacking in SD despite how often these terms are tossed around.

For example, let's take the term 'situational awareness.' Do you know that it's originally a military term? Or that in the military it has specific meanings depending on occupational specialties (MOS) as to when and how it's used? It's based on things soldiers are trained to spot and consider in their decision-making process. Situational awareness rests on a foundation *of clearly identified knowledge and resources*.

But the way it's typically bandied around in self-defense circles is usually phrased as 'something you must have.' At the same time, it's *never clearly defined*. The necessary knowledge it should be based on is *not* taught. (That's boring, not the fun stuff.) But boy howdy aren't they cool for teaching all that 'situational awareness?'

Quick... what factors and behavior do you look for in order to spot a developing robbery? List the behaviors. Which behavior is fake and what is unique to a developing crime? What strategies are common?

Do you really know specifics? If not, that's okay. Since most robberies are set up under false pretenses to lull people into complacency before the trap is sprung, it's critical to be able to tell the difference between legitimate behavior and trap development. That's one aspect of situational awareness for civilians that *isn't* regularly taught—if at all. Another absent aspect is: How do you tell when there is no danger present in an environment? It is important to know when to relax. Why? Constantly looking for ninjas or muggers around the next corner is a fast track to burn-out and becoming a nuisance to the people around you.

Mental models help you—a civilian—identify a dangerous situation and then navigate it. But the key word of that statement is 'help.' You still have to assess the situation, make the decisions, and put into effect your solutions.

This brings us to another issue: Is your map descriptive or prescriptive?

Often borrowed law enforcement and military models are descriptive. They depict a condition or something you already do. That's more important than people realize. Descriptive models are based on pre-existing skill, prior knowledge, and communicate shared standards. When you hear the term *you know what to do.* This is important so we will spend the time to discuss it because most descriptive models are about communication among people speaking the same language.

Let's use the defense readiness condition (DEFCON) model for throwing nukes at other countries. It increases in severity from DEFCON 5 to DEFCON 1. For the people in Cheyenne Mountain, DEFCON 5 is just another day at work (everyday activities and monitoring). DEFCON 1 turns another country into a sheet of glass. Here's the key point, the announcement "we're at DEFCON 4" results in behavioral changes and specific actions. When the commander calls for a change in DEFCON status, everybody knows *what to do* in those circumstances. DEFCON works in the military because there are specific responses and responsibilities for each section. They all work in tandem to achieve one larger goal. There is no question of what response is warranted because it's drilled into each unit over and over again ("At DEFCON ___ you _____.")

There are three inherent limits in descriptive models:

One, they communicate more than anything else, but *it's not full communication*. In real life, if there are a thousand men at DEFCON 4 most won't know what's happening. The commanders have full knowledge of the situation and, not the troops. Officers are trained to think under stress before declaring DEFCON. (Are you?)

Two involves the troops. There's no room for interpretation when it's time to act. Each cog has a focused function. These responses also follow specific ROEs so no one will be scrutinized for his or her actions if they follow orders. (You will be analyzed.)

Three, there are clear protocols about what to do at each DEFCON level. Officers and troops have external training in what to do (external in the sense it is not inherent within the DEFCON model). What to do is not built into the model—without this extra knowledge, training, and drills the alert model is functionally useless.

Is your map this detailed? If it's not, using such descriptive terms out of context and without a full understanding of all they entail doesn't help. It hinders. The map you need has to be flexible enough to cover other possibilities.

Are descriptive models useful for civilians? They can be—especially if you add extra training and more complete models. They're good for learning, but they don't do anything about your safety. Appropriate responses are not built in so you have to develop them on your own. This is made more complicated because we don't have a clear idea of what we're preparing for. Where things really go sideways with descriptive models is when people try to apply them as one-size-fits-all answers to violence. With the military that's the right approach. As a civilian you have different options, responses, and problems.

Prescriptive models outline *how* to act in dangerous circumstances. The instructions are *built in*. They also tend to have a smaller focus. They are about the actions and circumstances typical of a situation (e.g., don't run from danger—run to safety).

Since this is a new way to look at maps let's spend some extra time. A quick example of a descriptive model is Cooper's color codes. This was originally a map to mentally shift gears in preparation to use force.[20] Since that time many instructors have attempted to make these codes prescriptive by adding 'these are code red circumstances' and 'at code red you ____' instructions.

There's one problem. Remember the self-defense camps we mentioned? They all teach different definitions and responses. If code red means you fight what does fight mean? What does the camp you're in mean when they say it? They try to apply it to all types of violence.

Meanwhile, an example of a prescriptive map is:

---

20. White, yellow, orange, red are the "codes." Col. Jeff Cooper said, the color code as we preach it runs white, yellow, orange, and red, and is a means of setting one's mind into the proper condition when exercising lethal violence and is not as easy as I had thought at first."

- Notice
- Change the script
- If/Then

We'll cover this model in more detail later (to show you how to apply it to a specific set of circumstances). For now, we want you to notice you don't need to translate or remember what a specific color or tactical term means. This is instructive.

This does not—in any way—mean prescriptive maps are complete unto themselves. Just because prescriptive give you directions you'll still need to have extra resources, skill sets, and possible training to execute the idea. But you won't need to waste time to try to decide what course to take to get out of the situation. We don't want to go too deeply into it, but any prescriptive map's limits can often be overcome by overlaying other models on it to get a better grasp of a situation (e.g., *Notice etc....* with a threat assessment model overlay).

Navigation maps through potentially dangerous situations are *normally* confusing and rare. While you may have never been there yourself without a map you'll be lost. With such a map, you aren't completely lost. Just make sure the map you use is the one *you* need not the ones the cops, military, or samurai needed.

You can practice these models in everyday life if you continually notice what happens around you. This doesn't mean your head needs to be "on a swivel." The key is to pay attention when things look different because there could be an important reason for that. Or it could just be the local color and noise. But *you* need to be able to make that determination.

*Once you know they're dangerous,
they're not so dangerous.*

Quiz: What Danger Signs?

These are actions common to different types of violence. While a single point can appear in multiple types, some are unique to a particular type of violence. How many do you know and which type do they go with? Your choice of categories are robbery (asocial resource), fighting, ambush, or vendetta violence, asocial process, and multiple attackers:

- Secondary location
- Instructions to avoid violence
- Witness check
- Intercept timing
- Change of direction to intercept
- Silently closes distance fast
- Faux social script
- Hijacking of social scripts
- Monkey dance
- Humiliation
- Threat display or display aggression
- Often physical contact is threat-display, not committed
- Pincering, closing, pinning, or cornering
- Hang back then close distance
- Public
- Stalking, revenge, or backing up on you
- Fringe areas
- Isolation
- Criminal leaves
- Loser driven from area
- Develop attack range
- Too damned close

- Anti-camera approach
- Woofing
- Committed attack
- Weapon pat, check, or adjustment
- Take a position and wait
- Pops out of hiding
- Out of context contact
- Intimidation
- Wrong place or time
- Breaks the deal
- Return engagement
- Loiter and follow
- Adds demands
- Attack or stop
- Offer a contract, deal, or conditions
- No deal or instructions offered
- Renders you helpless to resist
- Weapon or numbers

How'd you do? Now read on
...

Violence comes in many forms and has different goals. These differences are why there isn't one 'you just do this" answer for self-defense. Understanding how crime and violence happen allows you to adapt to the circumstances and stay within self-defense parameters. Unfortunately, a lot of training instills responses to imaginary scenarios rather how violence really happens. That's why so much training fails or results in arrests.

Introduction to Violence

We've written this chapter for you to use for your current definition of violence. Everything we are about to say will make sense given *that* definition. By reading this your definition will change. What we can tell you is violence is a bigger and deeper subject than you think it is and means more than you imagine. It is a subject well worth researching on your own. After doing so when you come back to reread this book, this chapter will have new depths.

Too many schools take the approach that whatever they teach is 'self-defense.' The *first* component of self-defense, "understanding violence," is usually missing. It's impossible to come up with the right answer if you don't know what kind of violence you will face.

So with that in mind, we have a question. *Why do people become violent?* Simple question. (Think of your answer before you read on.)

Marc will ask a room of police he's teaching and get about twenty different answers. These are trained professionals, listing motives they've seen for violence. Here's the important part, they're *all* right. Until you hear many explanations at once, it's hard to see the common theme. But once it is spoken, it's a light-bulb-on moment. You understand how everyone can be right.

People become violent because they want something.

After that fundamental point, things start to get complex. What do they want? All sorts of things. That's why there are so many answers. Understanding 'I want' starts you off on the right foot. When people desire something, violence can be a way to get it. For many violence *seems* a fast and easy way to get what they want. The person who will go off no matter what must be dealt with physically. It's the person on the fence that you have a chance to deter or de-escalate - or you can provoke it. With the latter, your behavior will determine the outcome.

This pre-physical violence stage is commonly overlooked. That's a bad idea. Things are not cut and dried; there are a lot of variables, and these situations are extremely fluid. While you don't control the situation, you influence what happens—for good or bad. To help you understand how that works let's look at 'what he wants.'

Some people are testing the waters. Will violence work? If they decide yes, they will attack. If not they change strategies—but they will try to *threaten* violence first. Other times people will make threats, but never intend to carry through. This can range from a menacing look to a full-blown, screaming fit in your face. For others threats and violence become ingrained as their default when dealing with others—especially people they think are weaker. With others, physical violence happens so fast it's almost reflexive with them. (The speed they become physically violent crushes most of their victims.) Often people who seek to accomplish a goal are emotional. In that state (up to and including mentally unbalanced) violence looks like the only option. Other times things get twisted with revenge. At that point the assailant will initially back off then come back at you later—with a higher level of force.

But what causes most violence (and blows your self-defense claim out of the water) is when you become hostile when someone wants you to stop a certain behavior.

Again threats of violence seem a fast and easy way for someone to get what we want. We humans use threats *more often* than we like to admit.[21] We want the benefit of threats without the actual cost or risk of physical violence. But then there are some people who take it too far. They do everything within their power to convince you they will attack.[22] That becomes their default strategy. Some people do it out of fear, others from rage, many out of

---

21. Pay attention to how often our actions convey, "I'm not attacking now, but I might—especially if you don't change your behavior."

22. They intentionally act in a way that makes you reasonably believe you are in danger of immediate attack—if you don't do what they want.

wounded pride, several self-soothe this way, and a variety of other *get off on it.*

How can you tell what you'll face? Funny you should ask. There are a number of models. The one we like is Rory Miller's social and asocial violence. It's quick, easy to remember, and—most importantly—it's something you can apply in an actual situation. Is it the absolute last word that describes every type of violence you'll encounter? Not only no but hell no. It gives you a starting point, however, to understand and categorize violence. If you should ever find yourself in a vicious situation, it can keep your brains from blowing into a fine pink mist by your use of the wrong level of force. You also can better explain to people unhappy with your decision how you knew you needed to use that level of force.

Rory breaks violence into two main categories, social and asocial. Within each there are many different subtypes. You can bicker and squabble all day how they should be categorized and what situation goes into which subtype. (And many people do.) But the key points are that social violence is *inner* 'tribe' (inside the group) and asocial violence is *external* to the group.

That is a simple but profound distinction between social and asocial. It affects everything. The goals are different as are the 'rules' and 'scripts.' Something else that is different is the violence intensity including the objective to injure or kill.

This is a quick summary (for more information read Rory's work).

Social violence

While more common, social violence is painful, but usually isn't intended to kill or injure (i.e., require hospitalization) because you don't want to weaken your tribe by hurting your own.

Something the young, the selfish, and—apparently—college professors have forgotten is that groups *must* have rules. Certain standards must be met, and there *has* to be some kind of organization or hierarchy, especially in larger groups. Enforcement of group standards is social violence in a nutshell. Some reasons for social violence include rule enforcement, stopping unacceptable behavior, division of labor, and status. This is violence over group problems—including status *within* that group. Size doesn't matter; it can be a couple, a family, social groups, a neighborhood, or society's laws. What most people think of as 'fighting' is usually social violence. It also can be a form of punishment. But despite what social crusaders say it's not all about abuse, oppression, power, and control. It's *much* more complicated than that.

Social violence is filled with all sorts of off-ramps, ritualized stages, threats, communication, specific instructions on how to avoid it, opportunities to de-escalate, and—if the goal is met—physical violence *won't* happen. If the threats work and the goal is achieved, there is no legitimate reason for physical force. (This is an important way to distinguish what you're dealing with.)

Let's look at something that is confusing and contradictory. Tyler's story four *should* have been social violence. It—and we're going to have to go wash our hands for typing this term again—'should have' been just a fight. Because of booze, rage, or Braden not knowing better, he used a level of force that would kill or cause grievous bodily injury.

An important side note: we fictionalized Braden to exhibit a growing problem in society: People aren't taught the rules and limits of social violence, and yet *they still behave in that way*. Braden for example, drunk or not, never learned you don't try to strangle someone while pinning them to the ground in a fight—because *that* elevates the threat level to the other person (jeopardy). Because Braden wasn't operating within the 'rules' of social violence, Tyler's only choice was to use a higher level of force to stop the threat. This is where the confusing and contradictory comes in. You have to react to the *circumstances* not what you think should happen or what your attacker *believes he's doing*.

Asocial violence

Asocial occurs between different 'tribes' and species. Another way to look at it is asocial is what happens when that other person doesn't think of you as human. This goes equally for both types of asocial predator. Asocial violence is a complete game changer.

Rules change for the attacker and the target. The asocial predator has a different approach, intent, and mindset—speed and warning also change. Stopping him requires different rules of engagement, responses, and mindset than you who've seen or experienced with social violence. With asocial violence you'll face a higher level of danger, which requires a different response—including a higher level of force.

A big part of asocial violence is deception through faux social scripts. Pretense is a big part asocial. The situation seems like there's no danger (or that it can be resolved) right up to when it explodes. At the same time, what it takes to deter it is as subtle and dangerous. Depending on the type of asocial predator, the "instructions on how to avoid" an assault can be legitimate (and the consequences of not following them deadly) or it can set you up for a horrible fate.

There are two main types of asocial violence, *resource* and *process*. In neither will the person 'fight' you. His strategy is to overwhelm you to achieve his goal. We'll relay some insights to hold you over until you can do more research.

Resource violence happens over something that has a physical existence (e.g., your money, your wallet, purse, car, etc.) This is also where the interspecies idea enters. Wait, how'd we get from money to that?

Understanding resource violence *starts* when people kill animals for food. But that's why it's hard for modern people to understand the difference between resource and social violence. Most people are entirely removed from this reality of human existence—including what *not* being required to kill our own food has done to our psychology. (Historically killing a chicken for dinner was a child's job.) Our ancestors understood resource violence, without it, they didn't eat. They also understood the difference between resource and social violence.

Like any task, resource violence is about effectiveness to achieve a goal. There's not the Sturm und Drang common to social violence; it's not about dominance or 'teaching a lesson.' It's about getting a resource (in this case, meat). Or just as often protecting your resources.

Taking this up a level, back when most of the world lived in tribes or clans, people from other groups weren't considered fully human—therefore it was okay to kill them, take their things, and even enslave them. (It weakened their tribe and made yours stronger.) The idea that everyone is human and we *shouldn't* prey on each other has *only* gained traction in the last two hundred years. Even today, it's not a universally accepted idea everywhere on this planet. (Genocide, tribal warfare, and slavery still exist in many parts of the world.) Most of human history has consisted on preying on those *not* of our tribe. Muggers and criminals continue this tradition.

Someone who doesn't think you're human is basically what you're dealing with when it comes to a mugger *with three modifications:*

- You *are* a mobile ATM with legs.
- He knows the police will be looking harder.
- The consequences will be worse—if he kills or injures you during the robbery.

You can insult and provoke a resource predator to 'finish his attack,' but if he goes after anything other than goods or money it's *not* about resources.

About point three: Without hyperbole, it has become a survival situation.

Rory's original model was for resource predation. Marc points out that the other side of this is *resource protection*. That violence type is just as intense as a predator stealing resources. That's what it takes to stop a predatory attack. It's also an important element toward understanding the limits of self-defense.

This is a big concept so let's spend some time on it. Again, *most* violence is social in nature. How do you tell? Marc uses the wheelbarrow test. You can put your money, wallet, purse, or car keys (resources) into a wheelbarrow. You *cannot* put your pride, social status, emotions, feelings of being 'disrespected,' or enforcing the way things are 'round here in a wheelbarrow. If that's what the conflict is about *it's social.*

What you *can do* is climb into the wheelbarrow and sit down. Your physical body is a resource. One you have the right *and responsibility* to protect from harm. And that by definition is self-defense. You are protecting your body from injury or death—not fighting over an insult or threat to your emotions.

Under U.S. law life takes priority over property. That means you can't kill someone who is trying to steal your things (except for one funky exception in Texas). This gets complicated when you try to stop a theft or eject a trespasser from your property. While you can't shoot someone for *taking* something from you, there are complicated laws about the use of force to stop someone from filching your property. This puts you in a gray area between the use of force, participation, excessive force, and self-defense. You need to look into how the altercation is viewed in your state. Knowing this helps to understand the next points. Starting with the difference between theft and robbery.

Theft is the illegal taking of property. Robbery is the illegal taking of property through force or the threat of violence.

There are different levels of robbery. A significant number are committed with strong-arm tactics. Usually a disparity of force in numbers is involved. For example, three people surround you, putting you in fear of being beaten. Then they demand your possessions. Aggravated robbery is when they finish the attack (e.g., knock you down and rob you). Armed robbery involves weapons. In rare cases, they'll just come in shooting, which results in charges of murder, attempted murder and *then* robbery.

Most robbers stop at the threat of violence and will *not* follow through. Because deaths resulting from the commission of a felony are *always* prosecuted as first-degree murder (for everyone involved not just the killer). They can't claim self-defense if the victim resists. While robbery is a fast and easy way to get money, it's just as dangerous for the criminal as it is for you.

Armed robberies have a unique feature. The ordinary pattern of a *fight* is inciting the event, aggressive and hostile words, threat displays, instructions on how to avoid violence, more threat displays, developing attack or intimidation range, even more threat displays, and finally (if those don't work) an attack. The loser is often driven from the area.

Typically robberies involve pretending nothing is amiss, distraction via a faux social script (e.g., "Excuse me, do you know where Adams Street is?"), developing attack range, *attack*, *stop,* and *then* instructions how to avoid (e.g., "give me your money") violence. If these directives aren't followed, the thief finishes the attack. If the items are handed over the robber leaves. Robberies offer a higher level of force (danger). The ability to know when you're set up is an important skill.

It is almost guaranteed that violence comes with instructions—or an offer—on how to avoid it (Tyler one, two, and three). *These instructions are legitimate*. Physical violence occurs when the offer is rejected (e.g., staying when you're told to leave) or you somehow violate the terms whether implied or spoken. For example, you're told to leave the bar and you walk out with trash talk and the threat that you'll be back. With social violence these instructions are more of a 'change your behavior or there will be violence.' With resource predation think of this as an offered 'deal.' It's a "give me what I want and I *won't* finish my attack."

This brings us to the asocial violence known as *process predation*. These are the boogeymen everybody fears.[23] Serial killers, serial rapists, and chronic abusers fall into this category, but

23. They are a lot rarer than you think. While people are afraid of the idea of process predators, you're much more likely to get into violence over social problems.

it's not limited to them. The qualifying difference between this type of violence and others is simple. With the others physical violence is a means to a goal with this type violence *is* the goal.

The process predator means for violence to happen. It's how he gets his ya-yas. At best he looks for an excuse. In the middle he wants to draw out the incident and make you suffer. At worst he will try to take you to a secondary location to do unspeakable acts. The level and intensity of violence the process predator commits is far worse than most other types—up to you begging for death.

Often the process predator will hide his intent within social violence scripts (e.g., rule enforcement, status protection [being disrespected], punishment, and stopping unacceptable behavior). It's an act *and* an interview. As an act he's using social rules as the excuse for the violence he wants to commit. The interview is to see if you know what he's doing. If you do, *how do you react?* Are you terrified of what is about to happen or do you shift gears and use the force necessary to stop him? Return violence is *not* what the process predator wants because it will be a much higher level of violence and danger.

Process predators come in many levels. No matter the level a common strategy is to quickly use overwhelming force. Some cleverly hide what they are around those who can harm them and only reveal themselves to their victims. While many will withdraw when they see potential opposition others increase their level of violence. With all of them the question is: *Is he smart enough to spot when you're ready for him?* Sometimes yes. Sometimes no. And in some instances, the message you send doesn't register because where he's from danger signals are different. Other times, despite the signals you're sending he still decides he can win. Like so many other variables "it depends."

Another common behavior is when they think they are in control (have you terrified) they'll draw it out and play with their food. Spotting this is what we'll talk about in the "When the instructions aren't real" chapter.

Knowing about the social and asocial model, you're now ready to understand something you wouldn't have before. Social violence can *usually* be de-escalated. Asocial violence *can only* be deterred.

That's a subtle but critical distinction. Trying to de-escalate or bluff your way out of asocial violence is a green light for the predator to attack. He knows you're playing in the wrong field (Tyler story two) and aren't ready to meet him in his. If you do it right, you can deter most asocial violence. But sometimes it won't work. With some of these monsters, you have to go all the way. It won't be your call, *but his*.

Social violence still has many off-ramps before things get physical. With social violence you can usually talk down, reason with, work out, compromise, or—whatever you call it—your way to a resolution (even if it's you agreeing to shut up, behave, or leave). With that in mind let's talk about how you can screw up.

When you are scared and emotional it's really easy to make mistakes—especially with behavior and time. There are lots of implied behaviors with instructions (e.g., "Get out of here" means leave *now* and *be quiet* about it). When someone is angry, scared, humiliated and self-righteous they'll often blow it on these points. (This is important to remember whether you're given orders or giving them.)

There are other ways to make a mistake and get attacked. To name a few:

- Outright rejection
- Staying to continue the conflict
- Continued aggression while following instructions (talking trash as you leave)
- Passive aggression (As any parent is familiar with a child dragging her feet about complying while throwing 'tude).

The biggest problem with these behaviors is at the moment—and to your adrenalized way of thinking—they seem like the most brilliant ideas you've ever had especially when it comes to a last parting shot to soothe your hurt ego.[24]

Don't give in to this desire. People always ask us, "What if he follows?" News flash, Sparky. Most of the time when they follow it's because of your parting shots.

Peyton Quinn author and founder of RMCAT has Five Rules for dealing with potential violence:

- Do *not* insult him.
- Do *not* challenge him.
- Do *not* threaten him.
- Do *not* deny it's happening.

24. The other side is when you're the one giving instructions. Don't give in to the urge to get in the last word as the person is leaving. These digs typically bring the person back.

- *Do* give him a face-saving exit.[25]

This is a good set of guidelines (a prescriptive map). If you violate them, it will typically cause a social situation to escalate to physical violence. Rory upon hearing this model—rightly—observed that these *will not* prevent asocial violence. In return, Marc pointed out it won't 'de-escalate' asocial violence (remember... deter) but violating these rules with asocial predators *will* personalize it, and they will go off on you.

Take, for example, New York City actress Nicole duFresne. Her last words to a mugger were, *You got what you wanted! Why don't you leave? What are you going to do now? Shoot us?* It turns out the answer was yes. (How many of Peyton's rules do you think she violated when facing an armed resource predator?) You may not remember, but you've seen this mistake before. Tyler in story two was beaten and robbed because *he too* made it personal to the muggers.

Staying within Peyton's five rules also undermines a prosecutor's attempts to make it seem you were hostile and part of the problem. Following these guidelines not only keeps you from doing the dumb thing but explains how you knew not to do what the prosecutor will accuse you of.

Now you know social and asocial. There are many other violence models. Each has its own interpretation, spin, and definition. Like threat models it really doesn't matter which one you use, what matters is you have one. By having such a model you can begin to understand that *variations in violence require different levels and modes of response.* It's easy to spot the howling, threatening drunk, but a mugger who announces himself with "excuse me" is *far* more dangerous and harder to spot.

25. Marc adds a sixth rule, "Do not imperiously command." You don't scare off an armed mugger by acting like an offended princess or that he's an uppity busboy.

When you understand that crime and violence are processes with goals and predictable stages, it's a small step toward the ability to predict someone's next move. Like watching a B-movie, you know where things are heading. Unlike a movie, you can change the plot.

Violence Scripts

Generally a script is a protocol for behavior in a social exchange. Sometimes they are formal. At others not so much but accepted as "that's how you do it." The word *script* works because it really is like two actors exchanging set lines. Social scripts help us navigate our everyday world. For example, asking someone at another restaurant table to use their ketchup has some very distinct steps that you follow without much thought. If you think about it you will be able to identify the steps and the dialogue.

As silly as it seems *please* consciously run through this as an exercise. (It builds the foundation for things we'll talk about later.) Now contrast that with standing up, walking over, and just taking the ketchup without saying anything.

Here's a shock. Violence has scripts. But to see and know them, you have to know a little more about those scripts.

There are three important points about scripts:

- They work better if all parties are socialized to act according to these scripts.
- When someone doesn't follow the script, we feel flustered, confused, angry, or insulted.
- Scripts can be so ingrained that reaction to certain stimuli in a certain way is unconscious.

When we mentioned *robberies happen in reverse order of social violence,* we were talking about scripts. When you know what to look for they're as obvious as an elephant on a pogo stick. Scripts are recognizable, but you have to take time and effort to see them—*before* you're involved in one. Violence scripts come in many forms, but we're going to limit the scope to robbery.

In a robbery script whether you recognize it or not you are the star in a crime drama. You are being set up, herded, interviewed, and deliberately set off in a direction that reduces your chances to effectively react. For example: "Excuse me, do you know where Wilcox is" *is a false script.* His pretense of innocence sets off an insidious chain reaction:

- It triggers a sense of obligation to help someone because he asked nicely.
- It lowers your guard
- It creates greater confusion because you're getting mixed messages. (His words are a polite request, but his body language is predatory. And his actions aren't consistent with the way someone asks for directions.)

He's deliberately sent you down a path of social reaction from which it's nearly impossible to recover when he attacks asocially.

If you don't fall for this distraction and use the same level of deception in response, he's likely to break contact and move on. By *same level of deception* we mean: He's not quietly setting you up for a robbery just like you're not quietly countering his set up. Meanwhile you both pretend to talk about Wilcox Street. All of this while both of you prepare for violence, *but don't force it.* (He knows that you know that he knows that you know...) Marc calls this faux-smiling, tactical maneuvering "the Shadow Dance."

But before you can shadow dance, you have to understand violence and know the scripts. Those are critical to de-escalate or deter different types of violence. If you can't prevent violence, know *what* you face in order to use the appropriate force for the level of threat posed by the circumstances. It can be as obvious as to turn and walk away from what you've recognized as a trap (e.g., two shady-looking characters loiter on either side of a choke point you have to walk through). Or it can be as subtle as to stop what you are doing and—without fear—turn your full attention to someone approaching and say, "That's close enough. What can I do for you?" Another is while maintaining the boundary pretend you don't know the answer to the question or have what he asks for.[26] This derails the typical robbery script.

---

26. Common ploys to get close enough to attack are to ask for a physical item (e.g., a light, change, or a cigarette) or to offer you something.

Remember how we talked about how multivariable and fluid violence can be? This applies to muggers as well. Most robberies rely on deception and a pretense of 'normal' while engaging in some dangerous behavior (setting up the attack position). Bad guys rely on us to follow social scripts. They control the fake script to set up their attack. We take control away by introducing new variables (like not letting them develop attack range or position). This forces them to rethink their plans. Do they abandon their intent? Do they change their approach? Or do they try to bully their way through? These are important questions because by failing to fall for their trap, *you increase the danger to them.*

Understand, anytime someone engages in violence, there is danger *to that person.* If things go wrong, he may get hurt, maybe killed. He knows this. That's why an experienced attacker will try to stack the deck in his favor. If you don't fall apart and freeze—as he expects—and instead counter his attempts—it's a bad sign. A really bad sign. You've just demonstrated you're not as easy a target as he'd hoped. In fact, by shadow dancing (stacking the deck in your favor), you've just shown:

- You know what the game is.
- You probably have something up your sleeve that will hurt him.
- You're experienced enough not to show it.
- If he gets froggy, you'll do what you have to.

What he thought would be another easy mugging has become a crap shoot.

While he reassesses his plans, you might have time to leave. Equally common, you'll have to ride it out until he chooses to withdraw. Or he might just decide to do the dumb carrying through with the mugging, and you'll have to defend yourself.

The difference is now you've had time to mentally shift gears and prepare for that option. Use your words to set a boundary and say something like, "That's close enough. What can I do for you?" If he tries to weasel past that boundary empty your hands (drop your purse) and firmly say, "I *said* that's close enough. What do you want?" This sends a very clear message to the bad guy—mostly to find another ATM with legs. If he still goes, you've cleared your hands and shifted mental gears for what you have to do.

Robbery scripts usually start outside your personal radar (awareness) range. Radar is not just your personal space bubble. It is the distance around you that you are tuned into—especially when it comes to other people. In the city most folks only have their radar set for—at max—fifteen feet or so. In a crowded city, it 's less. That's to say *generally* you don't notice people and what they do beyond that distance. Most of the time other people are like traffic they're there, so what? Someone actively hunting has his radar at a greater distance than his prey. It sounds woo-woo, but once you know what normal radar distance is you'll be able to spot when someone has set a larger field than normal. A common indicator that a mugger is looking for a walking ATM is when he notices people from much farther away. When your radar is also farther out, you'll notice him too.

Another element isn't a script, it's the stage. Fringe areas (isolated locations in proximity to crowds) are where you'll usually be robbed. In a crowded city, there are still places where you are alone. Even if not utterly isolated in some areas, it would take between forty-five seconds to a full minute before you can reach other people or they are able to reach you. These are the *fringe areas*.[27] Think parking lots, parking structures, alleys, public restrooms, stairwells, elevator waiting areas, bus stops, and similar locations. (Start to notice how often you're isolated like this because predators seek those places.)

Fringe areas are different than secondary locations or complete isolation (those are *really* dangerous). While it's important to recognize when you move into a fringe area, it's vital to notice if someone is loitering there. Know that there is the normal act of waiting for someone or something (like a bus). There's also standing around not so much waiting on something, but possibly someone). Then there is predatory lurking (waiting for a victim). Each has its own flavor easily recognizable with a little practice. Be mindful when you see any of these behaviors in a fringe area. If he stays over there, no problem. If he starts moving toward you it's a bad sign.

Another indicator is predatory attention—especially to potential victims and in fringe areas. This one you have to watch because it's subtle and looks partially normal. How far someone's radar extends matters. In fringe areas, expanded range can be a point of concern. Anybody who is not good victim material will be mentally dismissed. The criminal loses interest and looks elsewhere. Looking away is a behavior we expect in the city. When

---

27. You pass through fringe areas. They're the places where there's not a crowd but could be close to a group. There are few people, but it's not completely deserted. These are prime hunting grounds.

a potential 'good' victim is spotted the predator focuses on that target (pays too much attention). Undivided attention on the victim isn't just abnormal behavior, it moves toward dangerous behavior.

Speaking as a woman, Jenna can translate this: *Normally when a man looks at you and you're not interested you can immediately look away (to the side) to discourage contact. That usually ends it. If you do look back at him—and not in an encouraging way—he'll usually look away. Matter settled. It's when he doesn't look away but keeps his gaze on you it is time to change the script. Go to another (public) area to get out of his sight. While there is a chance he'll follow, usually this works. If he follows and tries to make contact, then it is time to tell him politely and firmly to please leave you alone. If that doesn't work, then more firm than polite. If it still doesn't work, then you get help. Ladies, this script is not news—you already know this. Men, now you know; you're being communicated to from the first look-away.*

Regardless of your sex, this same gaze behavior in a fringe area is an *"oh hell no!"* moment. This should ping your Spidey Sense (gut instinct). Normal people wouldn't want to make you uncomfortable—even by looking at you too long. Normal people going about their day and who don't mean any harm are not likely to approach you in a fringe area. This is a place where personal space is usually respected. If someone approaches you, it means they want something. It may be harmless or it may not. Either way, it's time to pay attention and bring your threat assessment model online. Doing that when the bad guy is thirty or forty feet away is easier and safer than when he's within seven feet of you. It also gives you many more options.

Other staging is where you get variations. Has the mugger created a trap by positioning himself at a choke point people must pass through? For example, on a narrow sidewalk he leans on a building on one side and cars are parked on the other. With just a step, he closes the distance and traps you against a car. Multiple people can create a pincer you must walk between to move forward. With most traps, a pedestrian has to move into proximity to pass. Or is he on an intercept course? Upon seeing a potential target, the mugger starts to move toward where the victim will be. (Multiples usually start fanning out as they draw close to prevent escape.)[28] Or it could be a combination of the two. For example, someone or several people loitering by the entrance to a parking lot or parking

.28 Marc has a PDF about multiple attackers that has video links where you can see these setups.

structure level and following a person entering the area to his or her car.

The next is a collection of behavior displayed by muggers and robbers. This behavior typically happens as the distance is closed—*outside* most people's radars. They will happen whether you see them or not. One is the witness check, this is a fast scan to see if there are observers or anyone close enough to interfere. Two is the weapon check. That's when the robber 'pats' his weapon (maybe adjusts it) to make sure it's ready. Still another common action is pulling up his pants. When someone normally wears pants halfway down his backside, pulling them up is a readying for action movement.

We've said to get within range and create confusion a criminal will pretend innocence. This too is a recognizable process. He moves in a predatory manner outside a victim's radar bubble, but *as he gets closer* he shifts into an innocence act. You can literally see when he puts this mask on. This shift into faux-innocence is a serious red flag (jeopardy… big, bad, dangerous jeopardy). To spot it you have to have your radar bubble set wider than most people's.

Repeating ourselves because it's that important, this innocent act can be done in a number of ways. Some examples: He asks for something (often a physical thing to justify getting closer). He pretends to look at his phone while he watches you from under his eyebrows as he heads straight toward you.[29] Many muggings start with, "Excuse me." All are ruses to close the distance and disguise the set up to your attack. This pretense of innocence creates doubt and confusion that hinders your ability to effectively respond in time.

Another red flag is anti-camera behaviors. These approaches are more common in businesses about to be robbed, but you'll also see it anywhere there is video surveillance. The person turns his head and shoulders away from the camera. It makes no sense to move this way until you know where the cameras are. Another version is to pop up the hoodie and look down as he approaches to hide features and his ears. There are over twenty-five head and facial recognition points used by software. Ears are almost as good as fingerprints. These might seem like innocent actions, but in a combination of an intercept course and

29. Lose any doubt about this being a coincidence when you step out of the way and he changes direction to still intercept you.

timing (speed up or slow down to meet) they take on some specific meanings.

The next step is the interview. This is when the criminal double checks to see if you're safe to attack. This is an interview *you want to fail.* There are multiple forms of interviews (Look into Marc's Five Stages.) As we said before this is usually some kind of faux-social script while he double checks how dangerous you might be. Common to other kinds of interviews, he'll make a threat to gauge your reaction. Are you going to 'fail the interview' (which is what you want) or pass it? Ways to pass or fail this type of interview:

- Do you pretend he didn't say it?
- Do you get visibly scared?
- Do you respond insufficiently (which lets him know he can overwhelm you)?
- Do you try to puff up? (Which will justify his attack on you.)
- Or do you say something dangerous enough to claim he was just joking?

A key to interviews is what happens if the potential attacker doesn't like what he sees. Let's say you spot what he's up to and engage in nonviolent countermeasures or prepare for violence. He can abandon his plans and break contact—*while he pretends nothing is happening*. This 'safety feature' is another purpose for his deception.

> Important safety tip: This only works if you play your part *after* you've failed the interview. As he pretends nothing happened you should too. Otherwise you can reignite the incident if you insult him or act aggressively because you're adrenalized. If you do this you will be viewed as the primary aggressor. (After you're safely away, *then* you can freak out. While you're still in his presence, you have to remain calm and professional.)

The next step is range and attack position. In the previous section about setting you up, we discussed a general movement toward your proximity. This stage is the exact position he'll develop to attack you. Integral to this, he must develop attack range so he can control your options (the only choices he wants you to have are the ones he offers). There are multiple tactics an attacker can use. The absolute proof of evil intent, however, is the development of attack range. It doesn't matter if it's fast or slow, his moving close enough to touch you not only puts you in danger, but jeopardy (as in ability, opportunity, and jeopardy). An amateur attacker will develop range as he attacks (the charge). An experienced attacker will develop that range and position and then attack. While the former may cause you to freeze, the latter will overwhelm you—*if you let him develop it.*

Something we mentioned earlier: In robberies, unlike social violence often the attack *happens,* stops, and then instructions are given on how to avoid completion. If you're so far behind the curve you've let things develop this far, your best bet is to comply instead of trying to use your training. He came prepared for violence and has put you at a disadvantage. If you think you will instantly flash from loading your groceries in your car to that level of intensity, you're sadly mistaken. If you allow him to develop attack position and range, you screwed the pooch; don't make it worse. This is the safest bet because the last step of a robbery script is the thief takes what he wants and leaves. Remember all you are is an ATM with legs.

That's a robbery script in all it's disgusting glory. If things start to go off script, you have a bigger problem—it's the other type of asocial violence. If a robber tells you to do something, you comply and *he leaves*, things are still on script. If he adds conditions after your initial compliance, he is creating conditions that you'll have to fight for your life—especially if he tries to take you to a secondary location or tells you to do something that reduces your ability to resist.

An example of this is if he tells you "get in the car." You *never* go to a secondary location—*ever.* In the next few seconds you must do what you can to survive. Why? Experts disagree the number of rapes, murders, and beatings that occur if you're taken to a secondary location. Some estimate 90 percent, some say 95 percent, others guess 98 percent, but at that level it all sucks. They all acknowledge it is kidnapping, which, after murder, is the most harshly prosecuted crime. While that may be news to you, it's not to the criminal. So if a psycho takes you to a secondary location, it's not in his best interest to leave you alive. Are you catching on to how bad secondary locations are?

That is one example a violence script type; there are many others. It might sound like too much work to learn these things, but you will be hospitalized or put in prison if you don't know them or how to explain how you knew you were in danger.

*Situational awareness is more than a soundbite.
It requires underlying information before it's a useful practice.
Without this contextual knowledge, you claim to have scaled a mountain, but your understanding places you on a molehill because you don't know what to look for or what it means.*

Normal, Abnormal, and Dangerous

We don't have a problem with the concept of situational awareness, but we have major difficulties with the way it's commonly taught.

Of anyone who uses the term, we ask:

- What *exactly* is situational awareness?
- What are the nuts-and-bolts parts that make it?
- What are the standards?
- How do you develop it?
- How do you apply it?
- How can you use it to describe your decision-making process after you act?

These are basic and generalized questions. While you may have stumbled, we have some really bad news for you: It's appalling how many instructors can't answer such questions either. Yet they claim to teach it. By the end of this chapter you'll understand why that's dangerous. Like many other self-defense-related problems if this underlying information hasn't been covered, you will suffer—not your instructor.

The following sentence is awkward but very specific:

Not only is the underlying information important to recognize danger, not freeze, and not get your brains blown into a fine pink mist, but you must be able to articulate what you saw and why you knew it was dangerous to the powers that be.

Remember saying, "I was in fear for my life," in court *isn't* enough. You'll also need something more than intoning situational awareness to keep from being shredded by the prosecutor. Long before you get to court, you'll be in trouble for using 'situational awareness' as it's commonly thrown around and without context.

There are three generalized attitudes that accompany the soundbite version of situational awareness. Two arise from the conviction your training's effectiveness will cover failure in situational awareness.

First is the belief that when something jumps out of the bushes, you'll immediately drop into combat mode. A big part of this is believing you will perform incredibly effective violence at the drop of a hat. You don't have to 'be aware' because when trouble steps out of the shadows, you'll recognize it. With this insta-awareness you'll have the ability to flash into effective violence—whether that's a flurry of fists and feet or jerk your pistol out and start blazing away. This isn't situational awareness, it's situational reaction. More than that it's a 'Hail Mary pass,' and those usually fail because it takes time to mentally shift gears then decide to act. If you're attacked by surprise you're already behind the eight ball. It doesn't matter how fast you get your weapon of choice into the fight if you're already looking down the barrel of a gun. That's not an uphill battle if you try, it's a death warrant.

With a better understanding of your environment and how to recognize danger, you could have seen the situation developing while you had more options available.

Second, problems arise when you're so confident that you boldly walk into situations *beyond your training*. This is the ultimate in 'talisman thinking,' where you believe your training or equipment will protect you like a cross stops a vampire. Don't be so confident in your abilities that you *do the dumb*.

Don't willfully put yourself where if something happens it'll be beyond your abilities. Like the professional mixed martial artist (MMA) who drunk, alone, in a foreign country's streets, and late at night was attacked by five armed muggers.[30] The obituary columns are depressingly filled with such stories. Or thinking, "Because I have a gun I can go wherever I want, and that's all I need to be safe." Don't, just don't.

The *third* approach to situational awareness can jokingly be referred to as, "Be alert. The world needs more lerts."

If you ask "What's a lert?" you've found one of the problems with this approach. What exactly does situational awareness

---

30. Marc knows of such a case where the guy credited his MMA training for saving his life. Nope, we're pretty sure the credit goes to his surgical team—who resuscitated him on the operating table.

mean? Add to that: Awareness without knowledge is paranoia. This third approach's common result is you're always looking for ninjas around the next corner.

Common *within* the situational awareness soundbite is "eyes up, head on a swivel," "You must always be in condition yellow," or _____ (insert some other macho soundbite). We only need to address one to make our point. In certain circles 'eyes up, head on a swivel' has become the theory and practice of situational awareness. This is a gross oversimplification of seeing what goes on around you and that's *all* you have to know and do to stay safe.

While 'eyes up, head...' has a good but narrow useful application, it's not required twenty-four hours a day, seven days a week. It's a lifesaver if things are about to go sideways or have just done so.[31] Other than that, there are too many things to keep track of in daily life. Do you really need to know how many people are in the restaurant you just entered? Or who are potential assassins, waiting to spring into action? Probably not but knowing where the back door is located is useful if you find yourself needing to evacuate in a hurry. This means to do a quick once-over of the environment to ensure everything is kosher and then continue about your business. There is no need to constantly scan for ninjas under tables or terrorists having dinner before they shoot up the place.

These approaches are not applicable nor sustainable to civilians. You can't possibly live your life "eyes up, head on a swivel" or in "condition yellow" —as you hear over and over again in too many SD classes. First off, what do you look for in different environments? What isn't dangerous? What are danger signs? (Do you know they change from environment to environment?) Information without context is just noise. As we said earlier, awareness without knowledge is paranoia.

Here's something easier, more user-friendly, and you can teach to your kids:

- Normal,
- Abnormal
- Dangerous

---

31. A common adrenal stress reaction is to hyperfocus on the threat to the exclusion of everything else. "Eyes up, head..." is how you notice small things before an attack—like the guy's partner sneaking up on you. After the physical action is done, "eyes up..." let's you see his other friend running up to help them. It's a lifesaver in a bad situation, but while in a restaurant eating dinner with your spouse? Not so much.

This is a prescriptive model (it tells you what to look for) and a foundation on which to build actual situational awareness. Not only is it a critical tool for to assess a situation, it's a shield against the way a prosecutor attacks you. Remember the attorney pinging for weakness? Normal, abnormal and dangerous is your firewall against the most common pings. For example, when you say you saw your attacker "do a witness check," the attorney will ask, "How do you know he wasn't looking for his friend?" Can you explain the difference?" That explanation can spell the difference between conviction and acquittal.

Normal, everyday behavior, what is it? How do things ordinarily work? You'll find many of these answers in social scripts. If you look into body language, communication, and etiquette, you'll find you do know all kinds of 'normal.' The catch is it's subconscious.

You need to bring it to the conscious level to understand how much you know. For example, answer these questions:

- What is normal behavior in a parking lot?
- How close or far from someone do you stand in line?
- How far do you stand from someone in an elevator?
- As numbers increase in an elevator how does your behavior change?
- How do you handle it when you and a stranger try to pass through the same door?
- How long do you look at a stranger?
- How does someone act looking for his friend?

If you answer these questions in detail, you have a firm grasp of normal—*safe behavior*. People who go about their daily businesses in ways so common you don't typically register them. That's not the same as not seeing it; it's so routine you mentally filter it out of things you do notice. We all have massive encyclopedias inside our heads of what is normal behavior for different environments and situations. You use this unconscious reference guide to affect your behavior thousands of times a day. With a little effort, you can bring it up from your subconscious (where this information usually is used). An example of normal behavior is to take a step—back or to the side—when someone enters an elevator you are in. Giving that person space is a social script you follow without a thought.

Understanding normal is the baseline from which you operate in your daily life. This may sound woo-woo, but once you know what is normal for an environment something out of place will just 'feel' wrong and immediately attract your attention.

Abnormal behavior is a yellow flag that falls outside of normal. The key is to recognize when something isn't within normal parameters and pay attention. This buys you time to evaluate, allows for more options, and if necessary increase your safety. After you check out what feels "off" and find what's happening is something that has a simple and innocent explanation you go back to your business.[32] If what's happening *can't* be safely explained, you need to shift mental gears and prepare to act. This is especially true if the next thing he does moves into your threat model (like his attempt to develop attack range).

Dangerous behavior is all about circumstances that can and will result in harm. Dangerous comes in two basic flavors *conscious* (jeopardy) and *unconscious*. Basically, does the person deliberately act in a way to cause you jeopardy or is he just doing the dumb? Either will kill you but the way you handle it is different. Someone about to attack you is different from the idiot smoking a cigarette while pumping gas. The trick is to recognize dangerous behavior before things go sideways.

Dangerous (jeopardy) behavior is commonly wrapped up in abnormal (think Tyler story two where he is approached in a parking lot). That's why you must consciously know normal and dangerous. That knowledge allows you to relax around abnormal behavior and spot dangerous behavior designed to appear abnormal (as it sets you up for an attack).

For articulation purposes dangerous jeopardy isn't just generalized abnormal behavior, it's conscious behavior *specifically* targeting you. Dangerous behaviors are deliberate actions that:

- Can't be safely explained
- Can't be written off as coincidence
- Conform to known dangerous patterns
- Develop the means for a successful attack
- Adapt to overcome countermeasures (especially to avoid it).

32. Marc breaks abnormal behavior into three main categories 1) normal-abnormal, 2) localized normal, and 3) abnormal-abnormal. We won't go into it except to say that certain abnormal situations have scripts (normal-abnormal). These scripted behaviors indicate even though it's abnormal, there's no danger.

There are specific behaviors that stand out and make them neither normal nor abnormal. For example, a robber will enter a convenience store and pretend to be a customer. Customers are so normal they're boring. While there are a wide range of body movements—some of which are definitely abnormal—they aren't dangerous. We've told you some dangerous behavior: his putting his hoodie up *before* entering, twisting his body to avoid cameras—now add putting his hands in his pockets and hunching down as he moves past the height scale by the door. That is unique behavior that only means one thing—no matter how much he pretends otherwise.

Let's play with these ideas some more. Normally there aren't people in your driveway. But when you see someone walk up it, pay attention. While that is abnormal what are the circumstances?

- Is it daytime?
- Is he or she carrying a package?
- Is that person wearing a brown suit and driving a brown step van?

Then it's a UPS person. There is no danger, and it's not even abnormal once you recognize the context. This is what Marc calls "normal-abnormal." (It's a known safe situation, and you can move on with your day.)

While bicycles may be a normal part of the environment, that guy on a unicycle wearing a kilt and playing the bagpipes isn't. In fact, that's pretty abnormal. But it's not dangerous. If you live in Portland, Oregon, it's not even abnormal. It's a localized normal. That entertainer is just part of the city's color. It's all part of the "keep Portland weird" movement. (As if Portland needs to work on that... sheesh!) Odds are you have your own localized strangeness that's part of your neighborhood. If you think about it you have probably explained it to a newcomer.

How can you tell when things shade into dangerous? Before you can recognize this, you need to know a few violence scripts and have a threat assessment model in place. Say you have to run to the twenty-four-hour drugstore late at night. You notice three 'customers' who pay a lot of attention to you. A fast look is normal, extended watching is abnormal. As you buy what you need, you see them slowly meander toward the door. (This timing is abnormal shading to dangerous.) As you leave they follow you out. Of all the directions they could go, they 'by sheer chance' head toward you and your car. When you change course, they too change to guarantee intercept. These 'coincidences' have crossed into a robbery script—especially if they ham-handedly and covertly watch you in the store. They get closer and will arrive at the same time you reach your car door.

Given the totality of the circumstances, this is clearly a dangerous situation. It's too loaded with unrealistic coincidences, timing, and 'known behavior.' (Each behavior is a brick, it's the whole pattern that makes the wall.) Remember Tyler getting robbed and beaten in story two? Now you know all the things he didn't spot earlier.

We promised you we'd expand on the idea of prescriptive models. Now that you know normal, abnormal, and dangerous behavior, we'd like to share a prescriptive model that Jeff, Jenna's husband, developed. It's a process for you to distinguish between abnormal and dangerous in real time. (It also shows if a situation is dangerous or it's just your imagination.)

- Notice
- Change the script
- If/Then (The results of the last step dictate your next action.)

The following is the story of how this model was developed. Jeff and his son left a restaurant and stepped into the parking lot. A few steps into the walk to the truck, Jeff noticed a rough-looking character come out of the building and follow them. (Pay attention sometime to how often a person walks a different way versus the same direction as you.) At this point Jeff decides to 'change the script.' He changes direction by cutting between cars. This was to see if the guy continued on his current path (maybe he was parked near Jeff) or if he was following them. The guy continued on his way. End of story but not of the lesson.

Changing the script has many important purposes. It's a form of testing and verification. In the story, the guy continued on—proving it was just a coincidence. That's the test. If he had changed direction it would have verified he was following Jeff.

If the guy also changed direction to continue following the If/Then would have been different. Things would have shifted to jeopardy. This would have required Jeff to know what needed to be done to ensure his safety and shift mental gears to a higher level. Here's Jeff's secret weapon: He would have known the situation was dangerous before initial contact. (But since the rough guy didn't continue to follow, the *If/Then* was Jeff and son proceeding to the truck.)

With this verification process, you are not lost in your imagination or emotions. You have pre-existing knowledge about what it takes for someone to successfully attack you. You've seen the behavior (insert threat model here). You've verified it (made him tip his hand). Now you have consistent data to make a reasonable and informed decision based on high probability and knowledge of danger.

You've shifted mental gears so you won't be overwhelmed or freeze. Then there's the whole explanation to the cops on why your reaction was self-defense. If the prosecutor gets fussy and demands you be arrested, you can explain it to the jury. And sometimes when the bad guy sees you counter him he will veer off in search of an easier ATM with legs (saving you the tens of thousands of dollars needed to defend your reactions.)

Next, let's look at a situation that can be a little 'gray.'

Often people are hired to go through neighborhoods to distribute flyers. Very seldom do they knock on your door. While someone walks to your door, leaves a piece of paper, and immediately moves on is abnormal it's not dangerous. If a person comes to your door, knocks, and you haven't solicited the interaction (called for service) that's moving toward dangerous territory. While it could be religious solicitors, it's also a common method used to case houses. Burglars often knock on the front door (to see if anyone is home). If no one answers the door, they go around and break in through the back door. If confronted, they'll claim some service need (e.g., electrical or gas check) to try and cover their tracks.

Do you know how the meters are read on your street? In modern developments, meter readers drive down the street, and the data is transmitted electronically. Now for normal-abnormal. If you live in an older neighborhood have chain link fence and an alley, your local service people will drive by with binoculars. Unless you have an older system and a fence that cuts off vision, they *will not come onto your property*. Other than that, nobody has any legitimate business in your backyard if you haven't called them.

Answering the door to an unexpected knock is a crapshoot—even during the day. If you don't answer, people who case your home think the house is empty. They will probably attempt to gain access. Sometimes through the front door, but mostly through the back or side. (That's why the knock followed by someone going around the house *is not* a good sign.) Answering the door will usually result in some faux social script (e.g., a door-to-door salesman for some wonder cleaner) and the person leaving when you say "no." Other times, it could be a set up for a home invasion or—especially if you're a woman—something worse. (You can also check your town or homeowners' association ordinances to see if such solicitation is banned. If so, it's an immediate reason to call the police.

Jenna once opened the door to a nicely dressed man who claimed he was with the satellite tv company and 'noticing the satellite dish' asked if she needed service. He was politely told "no thank you" and had the door shut in his face. The next move was a call to the tv provider to inquire about technicians in the area. When they said that would never happen without a service call initiated *by the customer*, the police were notified. Her pro-Second Amendment (right to bear arms) shirt may have tipped him off that she also was armed—a prudent response for a woman and baby alone in the house when she answered an unexpected knock.

With Jenna's 'service call' experience in mind, know that home invasions are bad news. They are 'secondary' locations where terrible things are done without witnesses and beyond help. Many home invasions start with a knock. So Jenna's answering the knock (while armed) of an unexpected stranger on her doorstep *wasn't* over the top. You may not feel comfortable answering the door with a weapon (concealed or not), but it might not be a bad idea to have something easily accessible near the door in case someone tries to push his way in. Any of these answers pose a different set of challenges.

Or you can avoid it all by installing an inexpensive peephole in the door or a combination video, intercom, and doorbell system, which is worth the $200 or so it will cost.

In closing, we said we'd explain the difference between a witness check and looking for a friend. It's simple. When a person is looking for a friend he normally takes time to double check faces and clothing of people in the area (normal). A witness check is a fast look for the general proximity of people who might interfere or will be able to identify him later. He doesn't take the time to recognize anyone (dangerous). That's something you can easily explain to shut down that prosecutor's line of questioning—but only if you know what normal is and why what you saw wasn't.

When people pride themselves on their nonviolence, it's difficult to get them to understand how often they use the threat of violence to get their way

Threat Display versus 'Pre-Attack Indicator'

Believe it or not, humans are amazingly non-violent animals. Individually we don't even rank in the top fifty species that kill their own. Three points:

- Because everyone asks—meerkats are the most homicidal.
- Although we're not in the top fifty killing our own is a 'family' tradition.
- When we're serious about killing each other, it's in group-versus-group violence.

Turns out primates are the most highly represented biological family in the top fifty. Humans are social primates. (Hence the 'family' pun) One-on-one, humans are not usually killers. But there's a switch that's flipped in our psyche about group violence. Not only are we faster to kill, but it can be on a mass scale. Some perspective? For most of us, your cat or dog has been in more fights, killed more mammals, and survived more life-and-death situations than you.

Humans, however, threaten violence *all the time*. The problem is we do—and don't—recognize what we're doing because it's so ingrained in our lives it's rote. We give and receive threats daily so we don't consciously notice anymore.[33]

There is a direct correlation between our ability as a species to communicate and reduced physical violence. (Babies have to be taught not to hit, this works in tandem with speech development.) So how do we threaten violence? Before you say, "I don't do that," let's take a closer look.

33. Parents, think about how often we use threats to get our children to do things…

While there are small differences, two almost interchangeable terms are "threat display" and "display aggression." There also are different types of displays. Basically we send the message of "I'm not attacking now, but I'm really close—and if you don't change your behavior I might attack."

This implied threat of violence humans understand and use freely, if not every day. Every day? Yes. We're not talking extremes. Threats can be as subtle as what Jenna calls the "Mom Look." C'mon, you all know that look. Whether you were raised with it or still use it yourself, someone is about to get smacked. It's what made you say, "Oh crap! She means business." It works on children, husbands, dogs, and even fellow instructors. Jenna once kept Marc from cursing through a whole class by shooting him 'the Look' and pointing a finger at him. (Now, that's power!)

The difference is Jenna knows she's threatening dire consequences. Many people no matter how fierce, aggressive, or hostile deny that's what they're doing. Up to and including hitting people and then denying they did. Most often they'll get right up in your face and bark, snarl, and drool to show you how serious they are. Afterward, they claim they didn't threaten you. They also say they weren't going to attack—you just overreacted.

You can put all the lipstick you want on this pig, but it's still a threat. (As most people mean *threat* not the argle-bargle definition). This intimidation can be conveyed through facial expression, tone of voice, body posture, word choice, and range and often *all of those above.* Even if we don't use it to aggress, we display this behavior to send a message of "don't mess with me." It's conditional, but it's still threatening.

With this understanding of threat displays, go back and re-read the Tyler stories. You'll see them seeded in those tales. Information about threatening behavior can be found in books on body language, expressions, and animal behavior.[34] While there are some localized variations in general, this kind of behavior is universal among humans and higher order species. (A buffalo raising its tail and a redneck taking his hat off mean pretty much the same thing—time for you to leave).

Knowledge of threat displays is important because someone doing them doesn't necessarily mean to attack. They just

34. In fact, we recommend the works of Dr. Desmond Morris for a good introduction—especially *Manwatching* and *Peoplewatching*.

want you to think they are. So how do you tell the difference? Well before we go there...

A popular term to identify when someone is about to launch at you is a pre-attack indicator. Folks who throw the term around like to make lists of what to watch for (e.g., him balling his fist). This term and these lists are flawed for several reasons:

- Professionals and amateurs have different indicators.
- Different kinds of violence have different indicators (a fight versus a robbery).
- Different types of attacks have different indicators (a punch versus a knife versus a gun).

It's not a fixed list. Most people who teach this idea come from a particular camp and only describe how they attack be it with empty hands or a weapon of some kind. There is not a lot of overlap taught between camps.

The significance of an action is range dependent. One cannot attack until he is within range to employ his weapon of choice. So an action outside of its range... Often these actions aren't to attack, but to sell the idea that violence will happen if... You need credibility to pull off a threat.

- They work within the context and totality of circumstances.
- The 'bad guy' can still abandon his attack.
- It's playing the prosecutor's game.
- Most people who use the term don't understand threat displays.

The biggest problem when it comes to the way people think of pre-attack indicators is they want to skip over all the communication, threat displays (including how to spot display aggression) and jump to the rockin' and rollin' part. (That's the last bullet point.) Many people don't look for a threat assessment model, they want permission to act. There is not a simplistic list of "if you see him do this, it's okay to unload on him" Remember, it's the *totality of circumstances* that guide your actions.

A threat display *does not* give you carte blanche to launch a counterattack. At best, it gives you preliminary information to prepare for an incoming attack. At worst it plays into the prosecutor's hands. The same goes for what people call a pre-attack indicator.

Wait... what?

A common court room strategy is to sell the idea that no danger existed until the attack was launched or the second before the actual physical attack.[35] The problem is the way pre-attack indicators are typically taught focuses on the second *before* that attack lands. The entire purpose of this book has been to teach you to mentally shift gears and think of an incident as more than the final physical aspect.

We won't dwell on this topic, but there are a few things you need to know about threat displays, attack strategies, and threats morphing into attacks. First is how to tell if someone is threatening violence or setting up violence.

One of the most reliable ways to tell the difference between someone making a threat display and someone initiating an attack is *distance* (range). By attack range we mean he can effectively attack you with one move; specifically, he can kick or punch you without taking a step. A simple way to tell someone's empty-hand attack range—the distance he can effectively attack you without a step—is to visually measure the distance from his eyebrows to the floor then picture that distance as a line from him to you. If you are within this distance, you are in his attack range.

If someone *doesn't* have a weapon and yells at you beyond that distance, he engages in display aggression. Let him scream and get it out of his system, he's *not* attacking. When he moves into attack range that's when immediate danger (legal *threat*) develops. If you don't know about attack range, he can act faster than you can react because he has the element of surprise.

If someone is upset with you—or you with him—you need to insist on staying out of attack range. This can be difficult because our default behavior is to move closer and get more aggressive to better sell our bluff about violence. (We really don't want to be violent, we just want the benefits of people thinking we'll be violent if they don't behave.)

From a physiological standpoint, reactions take time and that can put you behind the curve. This is why furtive movements are such boogers. Waiting until you actually see a weapon pointed at you spells doom. The same goes for not being punched. Most people don't recognize they're under attack until they see a growing fist. By then it's physically too late to block.

---

35. Marc has encountered prosecutors who argued that even after an attack was launched, there was no danger (because there was no way to be sure the defendant would be attacked again).

From a psychological standpoint, this might sound stupid. People get in each other's faces to show how close to violence they are and they aren't scared of other guys. Most often they are in deep bluffing mode. Not only are they not ready to swing, but they so focus on selling the bluff they are caught flat-footed when someone takes them seriously. When they get nailed with a single back-off punch, they're shocked. (The fight starts when they get over the upset and charge back.) But if it's a committed repeating attack it's too late. They can't shift mental gears and get beaten down.

At close range, you can't distinguish what a movement means. Is it a threat display or is it the beginning of an attack? That's why you need to tell the other person to stay back (and you don't close the distance either).

Distance is what's important. It is also an indicator of the attacker's experience. Again an amateur develops appropriate range *while* he's attacking. (The wild charge everyone fears.) While an experienced attacker—who's far more dangerous—will develop range *before* the assault.

How to control the distance in a situation is something you really need to study. Knowing about attack range makes a confrontation less scary. Now that you know what he needs to attack, you have better tools in order to stay objective and in control of your emotions. This is critical to the ability to determine and use the appropriate response.

A lawyer will ping you for weakness on this subject—use of threatening behavior versus verbal threats. In a legal sense 'threat' has a lot to do with range and physical action. These are more menacing than verbal threats, which are usually all sizzle, no bang. You should know some common dodge prosecutors use to undermine your description of the physical threat is, "Did he say?" Basically the lawyer is selling, "If he didn't say he was going to attack you, he wasn't threatening you." This is not only wrong but deliberately confuses the issue. The danger (threat in argle-bargle) is in actions, not words. And you can recognize jeopardy through behavior.

There are many reasons why you need to be acquainted with threat display (display aggression) behavior. It's important in the three stages of an incident, which includes your ability to explain why—especially in asocial violence—the absence of threat displays before the attack was important. Knowing about threat displays keeps you from enacting them and sabotaging yourself when it comes to a self-defense claim.

Deliberate attempt to create 'reasonably believes'

What we're about to tell you wouldn't have been as valuable until now. Put on your argle-bargle hat: *People who threaten you deliberately try to create the reasonable belief you are in danger.*

The more aggressive, loud, and closer they get to you the harder they are trying to sell the danger. This gets tricky. To be convincing he or she must act as someone *who is about to attack you.* It's tricky because if you react physically, you're the bad guy. When you reasonably believe you're in danger, you're *supposed to* cower and let that person have his or her way. That's a win for the person handing out the threat. If instead you respond physically, the squeals start. Tearful blubbering of "I wasn't going to attack" and "I didn't threaten you" are typical scripts. These are especially common with folks who try to get you arrested for believing the threats they supposedly weren't offering. (Be aware that this dynamic is common when it comes to violence). If they can't win by intimidation, your arrest is their win by proxy.

Nowhere is this behavior more obvious than in people Marc calls "plastic berserks." Think of a howling, snarling, flailing psycho charging down on you. A real berserk is looking to splatter your blood on the floor—and unless you stop him he will. Plastics bark (volume), snarl (facial expressions), wave their arms (baton gestures,) and get up in your face (attack range). But *at the last second* they pull up short. Still in attack range, they continue to scream at you.

- This is deliberate bullying and intimidation.
- It's a rush for them (adrenaline is fun).
- This is what is known as *assault* in most states. (Yes, it's a crime, look it up).
- It often works so more people do it.

This behavior has spread from the poor and young into the middle class and supposedly educated.

Whether the person intends to carry through or not the behavior to put you in fear of an immediate attack *is deliberate*. This small idea has a lot to do with whether or not you stay out of jail. Until you've done serious research on the subject (like knowing about a conditional threat), you're better off not to use threats on others.

Can you tell if someone is drunk or high by how he or she moves?
Do you know how different chemicals typically affect people?
Do you know the drugs of choice in the areas you frequent?

Alcohol and Drugs

For a field that so often refers to the danger and ~cough, cough ~ unpredictability of high or drunken people, there is hardly any attention paid to how alcohol and drugs actually affect people. Want to know why this matter?

Do you know that alcohol suppresses higher brain functions? It *physically inhibits* a person's ability to 'think like an adult.' Hence the old saw "you can't reason with a drunk."[36] So do you know how to 'drunk wrangle?' Or do you plan to just use intimidation and the threat of physical violence? (Remember, kiddies, he's not thinking like an adult...) Worse if he's deep into his emotions booze removes inhibitions about acting on them. (Remember Braden's attack on Tyler?)

Do you know about the pain numbing and retarding effects of alcohol? Numbing is obvious. 'Retardation' has to do with slowing of the pain message. So it not only hurts less, but the message that it hurts *takes longer* to get through to the brain. With a drunk there's a lag time after anything you do. When drunk the average person loses coordination and these other factors also are present. A blow that would drop a normal person enters into a wobbly weirdness when the person is adrenalized and drunk.

There also are the walking nightmares. While there are no set terms for them, anyone who has professionally wrangled drunks knows about these people: *tush hogs*, *tusk hogs* (sweet little piggies when sober; wild boars when drunk), *perma-drunks, bottle coveys,* and *'professional drunks.'* These people have built up such a tolerance for alcohol they are still on their feet when normal people pass out. They are in 'blackout' mode yet still function. Although the term chronic alcoholic describes their overall condition and lifestyle,

36. ...but you can trick, lie to, con, and b.s. one.

there is a particular subset. When they go off they are—actual—berserkers.[37] They have no internal stops.

Marc worked several self-defense cases where the defendants faced murder charges because that was the only way to stop the bottle conveys from killing them. In one case it was deemed excessive force and imperfect self-defense. Yet, that was the level of force it took to stop a berserker with a blood alcohol content that would have rendered a normal person unconscious. We're not saying Braden was a tusk hog, but how likely was it he had the self-control to stop before he hurt Tyler? This was especially true in light of all the other lines he crossed earlier.

The same thing can be said about some meth addicts—hitting them doesn't work well. Now that you know pain alone is less effective on drunks and druggies, what techniques have you been taught that work better than a hit? Hint, the number of hits it takes to stop them makes it look like you're fighting—or worse beating—a drunk. As violence, booze, and drugs go together like peas and carrots why isn't this covered in your self-defense training?

- How do booze and drugs affect you?
- What particular 'poisons' should you avoid?
- What combinations?
- What are those things that bring out your bad side?

Forget, "Well I don't do those." Because even if you don't, this is a gateway question into something bigger. That is: *What's your internal landscape like?* Marc's wife Dianna has a saying, *Most self-defense instructors assume their student will be the good guy.* So too do most SD students. some questions about anger:

- Do you know what pisses you off?
- Do you know your anger process?
- Are you a slow burn?
- Are you fast to get angry?
- Do you let it go just as fast?
- Do you hang onto it?
- Do you like to punish those who dare cross you?
- Are you fast to confront people?
- Slow to confront?
- How much self-control do you exercise when you're angry?

37. In the Viking meaning of the word, e.g., shield biting, blacked out, rage killers.

These factors and more influence whether you'll stay inside the boundaries of self-defense or not. They definitely shape whether or not you'll participate in the creation and escalation of a situation and use excessive force. In your angered state, you won't think you did, but witnesses and video may show or report something different.

Just because you're angry doesn't mean you have the right to be cruel
Anonymous

Adrenaline

What laymen think of as 'adrenaline' is a cocktail of chemicals your body releases to prepare you for short bursts of action. We tell you *that* to put *this* in perspective. *When you're adrenalized you're on drugs.* Do you know how to handle yourself when you're 'high?' Here's the catch: just because you are on drugs doesn't mean you're *wrong*—or *right*.

Here is another important point: Adrenaline effects exist independent of emotion. But it is typically through emotions that we *interpret* the effects of adrenaline. That may sound a little 'chicken or egg,' but it's an important distinction—especially when we talk about fear and anger. Often emotions will direct our actions, but it's the adrenaline that turbocharges them.

Physical changes: When it comes to adrenaline and performance there's good, bad, but mostly *conditional* information available. Statements like "you can only do gross movement" while true for the inexperienced are demonstrably false for the advanced practitioners.[38] Adrenaline's physical effects go beyond trembling and wiggling your fingers. Something you should look into is the connection between adrenaline and someone's ability to take pain and keep going. Like alcohol and drugs, it can numb *and* retard the pain message—or it can make us hypersensitive to it.

Adrenaline not only changes us physically and behaviorally but also psychologically. Our perceptions alter (e.g., we hyper-focus on the threat). Different parts of our brain activate, and we—literally— 'think differently.' This comes from a time long ago when things routinely jumped out of the bushes to try and eat us.

---

38 Starting with the more experienced you are with operating under adrenaline the more adroit you become at that task. There are many factors in motor skill decay and countering them. Claiming you can't perform subtle movement while adrenalized is like saying you're forever trapped at Third Grade reading levels. It's not that black and white.

Adrenaline has a long history of changing our behavior by influencing our thought processes.

Under adrenaline's effects, the biggest pitfall is when it makes you think you have *no options*. You *have* to act or react a certain way or it's the end of the world. And of course, you have to do it *now!* Your emotions are screaming at you to not only to act but proceed in a certain way. There is *no doubt* your interpretation is correct and your course of action is appropriate. That's where wrong and right come into play.

Is that what is actually happening?

That's a simple question, but the wrong answer can put you in prison. (Think Tyler story, three.) Another way there can be a wrong answer is if you deny what's happening—usually by thinking 'something else' is more important. (Tyler story two). That version can put you into the ground. Going back to 'on drugs' adrenaline can convince you that you're in immediate danger when you're not. On the other hand, when the guy charges you adrenaline's message 'you're in danger' *is correct.* Threat models verify if the actual circumstances match what adrenaline is screaming at you.

Let's use a common adrenaline effect—spatial distortion—to explain the *what actually happens* idea. Marc often jokes he's never had a knife pulled on him or he looked down the barrel of a gun. He's had swords drawn on him and looked down the barrels of cannons. Once as a child, he was attacked by a sabretooth mouse. Is that what actually happened? No. But because of spatial distortion, things looked bigger and closer than they actually were. (Knives=swords, guns=cannons, and fanged mice...)

You are absolutely convinced the guy was *right there*, attacking you, and you acted in self-defense. Yes, he swung his arm in a way that looked like a strike, and you *did* see that. Except that the security video shows him eight feet away and *you* closing to engage. Are you lying? No. To your adrenalized brain, which spatially distorted your distance perception, you believe *he was next to you* and *attacking*. So that's the first answer to the question of 'what actually happens.'

What about the second version? The one about denial of what's happening—because you deem something more important. That's one most people don't think about. Adrenaline has a lot to do with how we react when we're angry and offended. A good analogy: adrenaline is fuel. It's not just necessary for your car to run, but how fast you go depends on how much gas is fed to the engine. When you're emotional, *you floor it*. If your pride is hurt, if you're feeling challenged, if you're outraged about someone's behavior, you can be so adrenalized that you don't see the danger. You can be so adrenalized and certain about what you doing the danger is literally invisible to you. That guy you scream at for offending you? He *is* about to shoot or beat or rape you. That's not because those his original plans, but they are reactions to your adrenalized behavior.

It takes time, practice, and experience to learn how to function under adrenaline's effects. For example, one of the ways to break its grip is with a fast measure-the-distance glance *at the ground*. We talked about how to measure someone's attack range. A quick look and calculation to determine if he's in attack range brings a different part of your brain *back online*. Knowing that he's outside attack range gives you more options. When he's inside attack range, it's time to adjust conditions. His attempt to re-establish the range is an important danger sign.

Sticking with spatial distortion, the effects of adrenaline can be turned against you in court. (This is why you must get the facts of being adrenalized introduced in your statement). A clever prosecutor will use the changes in your perspective as 'proof' you were lying. Proof? No. But you'll want to have an expert who can testify on your behalf about adrenaline's effects.[39] and explain the inconsistencies between what you perceived and what the video shows or witnesses report.

In only a few paragraphs, we've probably told you more about adrenaline's effects and complexities than most alleged self-defense instructors know. Yet we've barely skimmed the surface. You are not helpless under adrenal stress, but you *have* to practice to make good decisions. You aren't magically endowed with this ability. It takes deliberate effort to develop—especially when it comes to self-defense.

Let's talk about adrenal stress and scenario training. Hands down, we're for it—but with a few qualifiers. Starting with a prerequisite that your training is tailored to help you function while on an adrenaline high. If it isn't it won't do you any good in application. This concept applies to punching and shooting. For example, kata alone doesn't teach you an effective range of a move. Those old grips and stances in shooting often used while plinking away at a target might not transfer or be effective in a fight. Before you can act while adrenalized you have to effectively

39 http://www.nononsenseselfdefense.com/adrenal.htm

maneuver while not 'high.' When you have those down is when you move into stress and scenario training. Now about those qualifiers...

1. It's the difference between swimming in a pool and body surfing.
2. Scenario training isn't 'better' than traditional; both are necessary.
3. Have your skill sets ingrained before you try. (Imagine learning to drive starting with a race car.)
4. You learn how different training is from doing—and what you need to focus on more.
5. How to function under adrenaline.
6. You'll probably have to go through it more than once.

Tyler Stories, Five through Eight

Tyler Story, Five: Remember Tyler story one? The fight in the park? This time Tyler looks down the street, whips out his cell phone, calls the cops, reports the problem, and goes back inside to watch TV with Brittany.

Tyler Story, Six: In story three Tyler shot an unarmed man because he was adrenalized and upset. This time Tyler calmly accepts these things happen and his insurance will cover it. Remembering this he talks to the other motorist without blaming him, they exchange insurance and contact information, and Tyler goes his merry way to meet up with Brittany.

Tyler Story, Seven: At mom's house on Christmas Braden tries to get into an argument with Tyler. Instead of putting up with his abuse or arguing with a drunk, Tyler and Brittany go home.

Tyler Story, Eight: While taking the trash out Tyler sees a member of a group of young guys peeing on his lawn. Tyler shouts and begins to advance. Instead of zipping up and running (as is normal —and safe), the guy zips up and shouting insults. He and his friends advance toward Tyler. Tyler stops, pulls out his cell phone, and backs into his house while calling the police. The piddle-crew wanders off.

Happy endings, yes? Especially in light of the fact he spends time with Brittany instead of with Bubba in the county jail showers (and Brittany is really happy she isn't bailing him out of jail anymore).

In business, you don't get what you deserve,
you get what you negotiate.
Chester Karrass

Safe Withdrawal, Step Up, Changing Horses in Midstream

How much of your training focused on withdrawing safely from a potentially violent or an actively violent incident (like say, an active shooter)? Odds are your attention went to the active shooter scenario, but what is more useful is knowing how to safely walk away from a conflict and other violence. Why?

That's a really big question—relating to both soundbite self-defense and why we had to write this book. Many instructors in the self-defense field treat violence avoidance as 'fly-over country.' 'Fly-over country' is when people from both coasts skip all that stuff in the middle as if it doesn't matter. The fact that their coastal lifestyle is completely dependent on what comes out of fly-over territory doesn't even register on their consciousness. To them the only important parts are the coasts, they ignore the territory in the middle of the country. Violence avoidance is given ten seconds of lip service before spending the rest of the class teaching you how to fold, spindle, mutilate or shoot someone.

On the student side, there are fly-over questions. These skip all sorts of factors, variables, and complications. Yet the person who asks the question doesn't know that fly-over country even exists. To the student it's as if he has a map that's folded in such a way that New York and Los Angeles appear to be next to each other. Without understanding the subject, it seems to be a logical question because he doesn't know there's anything in the middle, much less that he's flying over it.

But it's not the way things actually work. You have to slow things down and cover the ignored territory because most of the time the answers live in that area.

Examples of fly-over questions: When we mention "violence comes with instructions how to avoid it and those instructions are usually legitimate," there's always someone who asks, "Well what if they aren't?" Another example: when we tell people "if given the instructions to leave, leave" there's always someone who asks, "What if he follows?" Most self-defense instructors will come up with some blaze-of-glory physical answer. They have just done a fly-over. They've also set you up to get killed or arrested.

As you read the rest of this chapter notice how Tyler stories five through eight apply. Let's look at the huge expanse of territory that's ignored... nearly 100 percent of the time when the instructions don't work or someone 'follows you'—it's because of something you did!

The ability to safely withdraw from a situation is a useful skill—even if it means "running fiercely," which it sometimes does.

Safely withdrawing consists of what you don't do. That's behavior the adrenalized parts of your brain screams you must do! We're not just talking about making comments about his mother's sexual habits as you walk out the door, we're talking about when adrenaline tells you that you can't withdraw from the situation because ______ (insert stupid reason here). Remember, social violence has many off-ramps to avoid it. One of which is if you control your pride, you can easily avoid violence. If you can't odds are you are part of the problem (which is why cops, courts, and society in general frown on violence and don't believe self-defense claims).

There's a lot of ego and pride mixed in with 'not backing down.' There's an old Irish saying: *Many a time a man's mouth broke his nose.* And this kind of pride doesn't matter what position you use when you pee; it applies equally to men and women. The most common and dangerous manifestation is when you see a potentially dangerous situation that pings your radar, decide 'they wouldn't dare bother me,' and walk right into it. For example, there are three dudes spaced out along the wall, and you decide you won't be inconvenienced by turning around and heading the other way.

Women—we're specifically talking to you about this. There are many reasons women justify why they don't change directions and walk directly into such a trap. Throw those reasons out the window; it is a dangerous situation

Marc's rant on avoiding violence for women: *The reasons to 'do the dumb' and walk into the trap are many. I've heard it described as 'I don't want them to think I'm afraid' (encourage an attack); "I don't want to seem rude (provoke an attack); 'I shouldn't have to change my behavior;' and—my personal favorite— 'They wouldn't dare. (Oh yes they would.) To avoid a dangerous situation by simply walking in a different direction does not invite attack. It is not rude. It is not disempowering. It's how to avoid having to gouge an attacker's eyeballs out with your thumbnail. Using nonviolent strategies to enable self-preservation isn't socially unacceptable. It's good practice.*

If Marc is done ranting, Jenna has advice for women to handle certain situations: *Because a stranger starts a conversation (or a script) with you doesn't mean you have to participate. It's perfectly acceptable to say something along the lines of "I'm sorry, I am in a hurry" and then skedaddle. First, this lets you acknowledge the person (because if you don't he or she probably will be offended, adding fuel to the fire). Second, it also is polite to apologize. And finally, it gives you an out. Respectfully and quickly take it. If he pushes it, there's another agenda involved. A shift in mental gears is needed at this point.*

Another part of safely walking away from social violence is to communicate that yes you are cooperating. Communication is important because—remember—when people are adrenalized they want it done now! Mixed with time distortion, they may interpret a second's hesitation as you not taking the deal. (You also need to watch for that or you'll pull the trigger too soon).

Here's a good rule of thumb: Don't ever run from danger. Always head toward safety (usually that means the lights and the noise).

Stepping Up (the other side of that coin)

In the same breath, we ask about withdrawing—How much of your training focuses on stepping up to resolve a situation—*without using violence?* How about effectively standing up for yourself without being obnoxious and hostile? Do you know the difference between assertive and aggressive?

Much of the behavior that causes someone to 'follow you' will make them take a swing when you step up to address the problem (Peyton's Five Rules). Physical self-defense moves aren't enough if you don't develop the skills necessary to handle angry, scared, and self-righteous people. You might want to look into this commonly ignored topic—especially the part about knowing when you can handle it and when it's time to call the cops and let them deal with the situation.

Changing Horses in Midstream

The ultimate fly-over question—after discussing withdrawing—is, "So are you saying we should lay down and take it?" (Or some variation). It's not that black and white. We're very much for people trying to resolve situations on their own. This so you're not used as a doormat and in lieu of running off to tattle. The tricky part is to recognize when a situation is beyond your ability to handle. Another challenge is to recognize what it would take is simply not worth it and it's better to walk away.

Unfortunately, you'll often find this out in the middle of trying to resolve something. That's when knowing how to withdraw is important, but before you get to that, you need to be able to recognize when it is time to do so.

For example, a drunk peeing on your property. The normal reaction when you shout at them is they scurry off. This scurry is especially common if, acting from anger, you are walking towards them while calling out. If that person leaves, the situation is over. However, things may not work out this way—especially if there's a group involved. If instead of leaving, they chose to confront, *you have a problem*. Certain individuals and cultures are very touchy about being 'humiliated' and will be willing to go to war over their 'right' to pee on your property. When you see someone start to react this way, give him a face-saving exit by you withdrawing (he'll think he's won). This also gives him/them time to zip up and leave. If necessary it gives you time to call the police.

Have you ever heard anything like this being mentioned in your 'self-defense' training? Because it is very much a real-life scenario if you live in the city.

Often the only warning you'll get
of a shark is a small ripple
caused by the tip of the fin cutting the water.

Finally—When the Instructions Aren't Real

The reason we've talked so much about this fly-over territory is because it's incredibly easy to slip into behavior that provokes people to 'break the deal' and not realize you've done it first. After all your pride is hurt, your scared, and part of you is screaming you *must* say something to convince him you're not a punk—or scare him so he won't follow you.

Remember our old friend adrenaline is still in the room. It's likely to distract you from your trash talk by telling you what you're 'really doing.' Things like, "you didn't insult him, you said that because ______ (insert justification for name calling)."

Marc talks about "a good faith attempt to withdraw." A big part of this shutting down Mr. Adrenaline. Pay close attention to what we write about trash talk while walking away. By trash talk and threats, *you* broke the deal. Aside from making the situation personal such behavior is *a known* danger signal in places where violence is common. Anybody familiar with violence has experienced a trash talker who leaves and then comes back to extract revenge. Often in the form of an ambush, but usually with a weapon or friends. That may not be your plan, but your behavior is *exactly the same* as someone who *is* planning to come back. You've made it in his best interest to follow you and beat you down.

The alternative is equally bad, but for different reasons. One of the reasons we've spent so much time on scripts and not blowing it is because when people don't take the off ramps (or let you take them) it's a bad sign. *A really bad sign*. Like shift your mental gears because there's something else going on—and it's probably wrong and dangerous. Chances are good you've come across a process predator. That's a level of ugly you haven't met before.

Process predators are the kind of problem you may not survive even if you do everything right. So to all the fly-over folks let's not be so hot and bothered to find the exception. The problems with process predators are:

- While not common in everyday life, they're more common in certain environments.
- They present as 'normal' until they reveal themselves to be monsters.
- They hide their evil behind seemingly social scripts or—worse—the false promise of safety.
- They're often like cats playing with mice.
- Violence is the goal.

Recognize that with resource and much social violence once the goal is reached, it's over. This is not true with a process predator. In fact the situation's perpetuation is one of the biggest danger signals.

We've repeatedly stressed that violence comes with instructions on how to avoid it. Often they're pretty simple and specific. "Get out of here or ____." "Shut up or ____." Often the threat is spoken, other times it's implied. For example, "Give me your wallet (and I will not hurt you.)" Most of the time these orders are legitimate.

When you deal with sociopathic (process) monsters the instructions get twisted (more confusing, demanding, and nonsensical) or are deceitful from the start. No matter which social script you try, the person *will* attack. He is playing a sick game that—in his mind—you will lose. Some, when you can't meet the unreasonable and escalating demands that is the excuse to attack. Others give you false hope with deceit to trick you into cooperation before they kill you.

The motivation takes a little explanation. It's not just that violence is the goal—they want to stretch it out; they want to see you think you have a chance; they want to watch the hope die in your eyes; they want to see your pain and confusion when you realize they lied, especially when they break the promise if you cooperate you'll be safe. That strips you of the last of your power and quite frankly, they get off on that.

Teja van Wicklen from *Mommy and Me Self-Defense* teaches about the false hope that serial rapists and murders often use on women. After striking her harder than she's ever been hit before in her life, the process predator apologizes for hitting her like that. If she cooperates he won't have to do it again. Believing there is hope for a social script she can use to keep from being hurt more, many women cooperate not realizing they're being set up for worse.

You should also know when process predators attack it will be with surprise, overwhelming force, and appalling savagery. The intention is to injure (if not kill you) but also make you helpless to resist. The only effective counter to this level of violence is to meet him *on the same level* and get there *just as fast.* It's go-time, and there is no room for error. There is no warm-up fight of punching each other—before you get serious. If you are to have a chance you must go from zero to combat.

Now that you know the cat-and-mouse aspect of process predation—and that violence *is* the goal—let's look at some danger signs. When these show, it's time to shift gears and prepare to go full force.

Goes off script

- That's now an obvious statement, but it's taken lots of pages to make it a no-brainer. here are some extras:
- Most people don't consciously know they're trying to follow scripts.
- When things go off script, they freeze or fall apart
- Consciously knowing about scripts keeps you from falling apart when things go off the rails.
- Things will go off script *at predictable times*. When you spot it, you'll know what to do.
- When you don't fall apart when he breaks the script a 'message' is sent to the predator that you know his game.
- People who know his game can—and will—hurt him.
- That is a bigger deterrent than any threat of prison or future punishment.
- You have to be as ready to let him walk away safely as you are to rock and roll.[40]
- If things kickoff you have to stop him immediately—otherwise you won't have a chance.

---

40 Have you ever heard your SD instructor mention this? Didn't think so. Not being able to do this is how a lot of people end up in prison.

- And you *will* have to explain to the cops and courts how you knew what you used was the necessary level of force.

Breaks the contract or adds conditions (stacks demands)

These usually come in combination but can be done individually. It can be outright breaking the deal *or* extending the length of the incident by adding new instructions. *Both are bad.*

If—for example—the instruction was to shut up, but there was no order to leave if you don't say anything, aren't glaring at him, and he tries to smack you—*he's* escalating things. Another example, it is not uncommon in the rougher part of town for people to follow you to the door and watch to make sure you don't go to your car to get a weapon, but they typically hang back. You don't need an escort, and they certainly have no business closing the distance once you're out of sight of other people.

The same goes for stacking demands. It's *not* a one and done. First it was this, then it's that, then it's…

Remember the idea with a process predator is to see how long he can keep you dancing on the string (hoping to avoid violence) before he attacks. While added conditions alone are not a good sign, they often go hand-in-hand with the next point.

Humiliation

This one takes a little clarification. Ego, pride, adrenaline, and parts of your brain will tell you you're being humiliated by getting instructions to avoid violence. It's really not. As mentioned, these instructions are often really simple. Like 'shut up' or 'leave.' You may not like the tone, you may feel disrespected that someone is talking to you like that, but that's *not* him debasing you—that's *you* interpreting it as humiliation. There's a simple way to tell the difference.

You should never have to crawl on your hands and knees, bark like a dog, or perform degrading acts to avoid being beaten. If that's the added condition, he's humiliating you.

Secondary location

Reminder: if anyone is killed during the commission of a violent felony, charges automatically go to murder one for everyone involved. *Criminals know this.* (And this is part of the reason you really want to watch the idiots who don't just threaten violence but start a robbery by knocking people around.) In the same vein, forcing someone to move during a robbery can be prosecuted as kidnapping. They know that too. They also know that kidnapping is prosecuted almost as fiercely as murder.

Consequently, there is *nothing good* that can come if you allow yourself to be taken to a secondary location—especially an isolated area. (Social violence often happens in front of witnesses, asocial in isolation).

Reduce your ability to resist

Remember the robbery script of rob and leave? He *doesn't* need to tie you up so he can make his getaway.

There's no need for you to get in the trunk of the car either.

Conclusion

You now know what really lives in the question of 'what if the instructions...'

It ain't pretty.

Yes, these monsters exist and, *to the average person,* they are beyond dangerous. They will use a level of violence it's hard for most people to imagine. Process predators are rare but require a much higher level of force to effectively deal with them. How rare? Most people will never encounter one.

Instructors don't make money, however, by telling you how rare the boogeyman is. They make their cash by telling you you're 'prepared' to face monsters. You're not.

If you ever meet a process predator you *do* need to know how to deal with him. At the same time, you can't assume that every attacker is the boogeyman. You need to be able to discern between a guy who's pissed off at you versus the robber who wants to make a withdrawal from the ATM on legs or the sociopath who will rape and kill you.

The only defense against evil,
violent people is good people
who are more skilled at violence.
Rory Miller

Bits and Bobs

Now that you know more about the way violence happens than you did before, we have some extra points to consider. This is a grab-bag of a chapter. These points are worth looking into but don't clearly fit elsewhere.

Freeze or Stop

A lot of people are concerned about freezing when it's time to act. Believe it or not, we've given you all kinds of tools to break the freeze. The biggest is recognizing when you're in a potentially violent situation and 'shifting gears.' The second is to not let someone develop attack range. It's hard to catch up when the first indication you're under attack is when you look down the barrel of a gun or see a fist grow bigger.

The other thing you need to look into is learning how to stop. Yeah, yeah, break the freeze. Great. Except what will torpedo your self-defense claim is when you chase the guy down the street, beating him from behind. Think we're making this up? A.D.R.E.N.A.L.I.N.E. Yes that wonderful stuff that tells you what a great idea it is to chase him or kick him when he's down because he might try to get up. (Or do you want to punish him?) The term for that is *excessive force…* if not manslaughter.

Size Matters (as Do Numbers)

How much bigger and heavier does someone have to be before you know you can't take him in a head-to-head slugfest? If you know this limitation exists:

- Why aren't you training for it?

- Why are you taking a martial art that encourages you to go head on with someone bigger than you?
- Why aren't you being taught to handle people of different sizes?

Going head-to-head with a bigger person will get you flattened. Are you listening, ladies? If you're bigger and stronger, you will be attacked differently by a smaller person who is accustomed to going up against larger people. If a small female is taught to fight the same way as larger men, she is set up to fail.

> Important safety tip: A smaller person who isn't afraid to fight a larger person is more likely to know effective moves to use against bigger opponents than bigger people are to know what works best against a smaller person. This includes knowledge of how to counter common 'big person' strategies.

What's your stop counting and start running number? It's kind of important to have that figured out before you find yourself in such a situation. Oh, and while we're at it: Has anyone taught you the common tactics of multiple attackers and what these setups look like? Or has all your training been oriented to fight one attacker at a time like a cheap action flick? Here's a hint about multiple attackers, the guy talking is usually the *distraction*. Ever heard that before? If not, why not? Again, it's not your fault, but it is—very much—your problem.

Brandishing Laws

Do you carry a knife or a gun for self-defense? First, if it's a knife *stop that*. Not carrying but telling everyone you have it for 'self-defense.' A knife is a tool. That's why you have it. And ditch anything marketed as a 'fighting' knife or 'tactical.'

What do you know about the *brandishing* (a deadly weapon) or *felony menacing* laws in your state? This is kind of important because often if you pull a weapon to defend yourself, your attacker will change his mind and stop his immediate threat. Great! You didn't have to hurt anyone. Yay! Except if someone calls the cops—including the guy who threatened you—they will show up, looking for the crazy person they got a complaint about who was waving around a weapon. You'd better be able to explain why you pulled it and why you didn't use it—or you'll face brandishing charges.[41]

What's Your Strategy for Different Ranges?

The last time Marc was shot at, the shooter was across the street in an idling car. Yet many a time he ended up on the ground *with* someone meaning to do him harm. Does your training cover what's required at different distances? Many martial artists don't know the difference between cover and concealment. Many shooters have no answer to "what's your defensive action against someone trying to stab you?" (Hint: pulling the trigger won't stop the blade from entering your guts.)

Often people who come for self-defense training want one answer that works at *all* ranges. Unfortunately there are many instructors who will sell them what they want to hear. Just knowing that different distances require different priorities and strategies will keep you from falling for these lies.

Has your training covered what to do when you're ambushed? You know, the guy seeking vengeance who steps out of the shadows as you unlock your front door or car? Way too many people think in terms of counterattack, but you're better off doing something that moves you offline and buys you time. Better yet has your training covered how to spot where a stalker would wait? (Survival is easier if you spot him from a distance.)

What's Your Ground Game?

We're not going to suggest you go out and earn a black belt in Brazilian Jiu-Jitsu (a form of wrestling). But slipping, falling, being dragged over, tackled, and knocked down is common during violence—especially when you're tangled up with an assailant. What have you done to address that issue?

While "90 percent of all fights go to the ground" is pure marketing BS, it's not an exaggeration to say nearly 100 percent of all deaths from bare hands happen on the ground. A majority of these arise from one simple cause: *Most people don't know how to correctly fall.* That results in their falling and cracking their skulls open. Even if that doesn't happen when you get knocked over and hit your head, you would be stunned and would have a hard time

---

41 What does your instructor say about calling the cops after an incident? Do you know there's a hot debate about that? If not, research it. If yes, there's absolute answer. You need to look into it more.

rallying. You may not be helpless, but you'll definitely be behind the curve. Do you know how to fall so you don't get the wind knocked out of you, hit your head, or break something? Breaking or spraining something are more common results than dying. (Hint: It's hard to draw your gun with a broken wrist.)

Now that you've survived the fall do you know how to 'handle yourself on the ground?' You don't have to be a black belt in a ground-fighting system, but it helps to have a working strategy for self-defense and *getting back up*—not submission fighting.

If a gun is your tool of choice did you know that you can shoot from the ground? It may not seem intuitive, but if you find yourself in a position of disadvantage doesn't mean you have to roll over and die.

This might not occur to you if you haven't thought about it before it happens.

You have to learn it—safely.

You have to practice—safely.

We highly recommend training on shooting from different disadvantageous positions. (Getting stomped to death isn't hyperbole.) It would be great to have these skills in your toolbox if you ever need them.[42]

Here's another consideration: Have you looked into a way to get up from the ground while someone is trying to kick in your teeth? Having to fend off incoming attacks while trying to get up is a real-life problem. Many people who don't know the problem exists discover they have no solution when it happens. Consequently they get stomped.

Time and Resources

These are way past the introductory scope of this book. While not necessarily covered in training, they are critical in the application. Why critical? In the extreme, they are life-saving or life-taking factors you need to accurately assess at the time with a fast glance.

Time - Do you have time to deploy your preferred response? Or is something else required first? For example, don't waste precious seconds using two hands to draw your concealed pistol when someone is swinging a meat cleaver at you. (As Terry Trahan

---

42 From Jenna: *Please find someone qualified to help you work through this. It is super easy to be unsafe while working on these things. For instance, just because you are on the ground doesn't mean that you can point a gun in an unsafe direction). Most instructors don't or won't or can't teach this.*

says, "You have to fight for your draw.") If you don't address the incoming danger at best all you do is trade fatal damage.

Resources - Yep, you're a trained mixed martial artist. Can you take on four armed guys? Especially when you discover they're armed after you've decided to fight them.

These are real-life problems, but often training takes the fantasy route. Some guy swinging a meat cleaver at you? The answer is to get your gun out faster and start shooting. That'll keep that nasty cleaver from splitting your skull. Armed muggers? We teach you how to fight multiples and deal with weapons when all you have is your bare hands.

If you have more than six months of self-defense 'training' and the concepts of time and resources are new to you, you have problems with your training's quality.

Escape, Evasion, and Withdrawal

How much have you looked into about getting *out* of dangerous situations?

- Not just running fiercely, but do you look for escape routes when you first enter an area?
- Do you know how to safely get out of a place?
- What about getting to safety when there are bullets in the air?

Bailsman and Lawyers

What do you know about choosing a good lawyer and bail bondsman? You might want to do a little research into these subjects. When you need one is not the time to start looking into this subject. We recommend you look into the debate about having an attorney on retainer or not. Then make an informed decision that is right for you.

Once you know they're dangerous—they're not so dangerous.

Remember that Quiz?

Several chapters ago we gave you a jumbled list of strange terms. Now they should be easily recognizable and the following categorization will make sense:

Crime

- Isolation
- Faux social script
- Fringe areas
- Loiter and follow
- Change of direction to intercept
- Intercept timing (speed up or slow down)
- Witness check
- Weapon pat, check, or adjustment
- Anti-camera approach (turn head, hoodie)
- Develop attack range
- Too damned close
- Out-of-context contact (verbal or touch)
- Pincering, closing, pinning, or cornering
- Attack or stop
- Instructions to avoid completion of violence
- Criminal leaves
- Take a position and wait
- Offer a contract, deal, or conditions
- Weapons or numbers

Fighting

- Woofing
- Intimidation

- Monkey dance
- Threat display or display aggression
- Public (can happen anywhere)
- Instructions to avoid
- Often physical contact is a threat display, not committed (finger poke, shove back, or hit and step back)
- Develop attack range
- Offer a contract, deal, or conditions
- Committed attack by both parties\
- Social violence rules
- Loser driven from area

Ambush or Vendetta Violence

- Stalking, revenge, or backing up on you (after seeming to take a deal)
- Take a position and wait
- Fringe areas
- Isolation
- Witness check
- Weapon pat, check, or adjustment (or in hand)
- Silently closes distance fast
- Pops out of hiding Wrong place or time (e.g., on your property at night or in your house)
- No deal or instructions offered
- Weapon or numbers
- Develop attack range
- Committed attack by ambusher (savage violence meant to injure or avenge a 'wrong')
- Intercept timing
- Return engagement
- Pincering, closing, pinning, or cornering

Asocial (process)

- Breaks the deal
- Faux social script
- Hijacking of social scripts (looks like other types)

- Adds demands
- Hang back then close distance
- Out of context contact (pre-rape touch)
- Isolation
- Develop attack range
- Secondary location
- Humiliation
- Renders you helpless to resist
- Committed attack

Multiple Attackers

- Instructions to avoid
- Change of direction to intercept
- Hijacking of social scripts
- Pincering, closing, pinning, or cornering
- Hang back then close distance (slowly develop range then attack)
- Public (can happen anywhere)
- Stalking, revenge, or backing up
- Develop attack range
- Numbers
- Committed attack
- Return engagement
- Loiter and follow
- No deal or instructions offered
- Renders you helpless to resist

Now you know how to identify what you may face. This helps you react appropriately and justify yourself afterward. You also can practice by watching YouTube videos of crime and violence to better identify these situations.

Tyler Story, Nine

Remember the Tyler who didn't know this stuff? He's back. He's in the parking lot after the fender bender. This time he doesn't have a gun. He's a martial artist and the other guy blows his stack and swings at Tyler. In a blaze of kung fu prowess, Tyler hits the guy hard enough to break his jaw. The man falls; Tyler leaves. Later the police show up at his home and arrest him (a parking lot video showed his license plate). He is charged with aggravated assault. Thinking he acted in self-defense, Tyler doesn't take the plea. In fact, he's told his attorney he wants to tell his story. Now he's sitting on the stand being cross-examined by the prosecutor.

Here is a list of questions the prosecutor will use to try to trip him up:

- Were you angry?
- Why didn't you leave before it got physical?
- Did you admit fault in the accident?
- Did you provoke him?
- He says you…
- The video shows you approached him did you intend to teach him a lesson?
- How did you know he was attacking?
- Why didn't you use less force?
- Don't you train to beat someone up?
- Weren't you just itchin' to use that training?
- Did you mean to maim him?
- Did you not worry about the fact you had maimed a man?
- Why'd you leave the scene?
- Isn't it true that you left because you knew you committed a crime?
- Why didn't you call the cops?
- Isn't it true that you felt good about hurting your fellow citizen?
- And many, many more...

Tyler had better have answers to these questions. Because if he fumbles on any one, the prosecutor will come in through that weakness like an attacking shark and will tear him up.

Once you are in the territory of a predatory prosecutor, they all want their meal.
John Curley

Pinging for Weaknesses

The authors have experience making statements to the police, giving depositions, and sitting in the witness stand. We both can tell you, "It's not an interview; it's an interrogation." An interrogation with the goal of making you admit you did something wrong. Even if that's *not what happened.* (Look at what the prosecutor did to Tyler.) It's an interrogation to trip you up and make you look like a liar.

We've spent a lot of time covering what you need to know about how to use appropriate force or make the decision to scale the force you use up or down. Let's look at what happens when you're grilled and have to justify what you did. Remember if you claim what you did was in self-defense, you have to make a statement. If not at the scene, later. You also have to know what information is imperative to share at the scene. Memorizing a script of what to say to the cops (or worse reading it from your concealed carry insurance card) will not cut it. (That reeks of premeditation.

The higher the level of force involved, the more you're going to need to have your lawyer present. If while explaining a lower force incident you sense things turning against you, it's time to shut up and bring in counsel. This includes telling the cops you'll finish your statement in the presence of your attorney. This is not the same as 'shut up and lawyer up.' (See point three).

In tandem with the high level of force, the first person you have to convince what you did was in self-defense is your attorney. This will not go well for you if you are unable to explain to your lawyer why your actions were appropriate. He's on your side, the other people asking questions won't be.

People unhappy with your use of force will ask you questions designed to trip you up. Not only can they make false claims to get a negative reaction, but they will spin their questions to make you admit to doing something wrong. (Look up the Reid

Technique.) This is another reason why you have to know the boundaries of self-defense. If they ask a question that will make you look bad, you must be able to answer why it was an appropriate move in the context of self-defense.

They'll ask questions to cast your actions—if not character—in the most negative light possible. A real-life example of this was when Jenna had to defend her profession on the witness stand. "While testifying in a case, it was brought up by the opposing counsel that I was a firearms instructor. The attorney asked me if it was true that I taught people to kill others for a living." Even if they don't work, these kinds of questions serve another purpose. They shock and fluster you. When you're flustered you are more likely to get angry, make mistakes, and fall for their next word trap.

They'll ask seemingly reasonable questions to make it seem like you're lying. For example, when adrenalized you focus on the threat. You—literally—don't see other things. This gets awkward if you are asked about something that sounds like you should have seen. Marc describes this strategy as the "I find it hard to believe you didn't see the elephant standing in plain view." If you didn't see it admit you didn't. But remind them why; "I was too focused on the charging tiger."

They'll try to undermine what you did see. If you can articulate that what you saw was dangerous, they'll go after you with "how do you know it wasn't something else?" This is where being able to explain normal, abnormal, and dangerous comes in. Any term you use you must defend. Remember the example if you say "witness check" the attorney will ask how you know he wasn't looking for a friend?" Do you remember the answer? Can you come up with it right now? (Hint: Looking for a friend is a slower, more deliberate action…)

When they've switched to 'building a case against you' mode, cops—deliberately—won't ask questions that will exonerate you. While this game starts with police interrogation, it comes into full bloom in the courtroom. They want to stonewall as much exculpatory evidence as possible. That means they're going to carefully ask questions they can use to indict you, but not ask questions that will make it hard to convict you. This is a long-term strategy because the prosecution will attempt to rule out any positive evidence that was not covered in your original statement or the police report.

A critical subset, especially with higher use-of-force incidents, is why you want to make a statement at the station and while being filmed. If it's in your original statement, they're stuck dealing with it. This subset is about what isn't put into a written police report. It is an old before video trick (and it happens these days with 'malfunctioning' body cams and small-town police forces). Important things you say that prove it was self-defense, somehow don't get into the written report.

Many police cars have recording equipment in them. Unless you want what you say in the back seat of the cruiser to be admissible in court, we recommend you keep your mouth shut. This is easier said than done because of Mr. Adrenaline. The same goes for spontaneous utterances in the emergency room and booking. (And a bit of extra advice—don't talk to anybody in the holding cells. To get time off their sentences, jailhouse snitches will make up stories about how you confessed. All it takes is a mute video of you and him talking—even if you were just exchanging recipes. A full confession of your crime isn't likely if the video shows the conversation only lasting long enough for you to say "Excuse me. I can't talk to you. I'm waiting for my lawyer.")

Speaking of Mr. Adrenaline...

If you are a good guy who acted in self-defense your first reaction is to tell Officer Friendly everything that just happened. You are after all the good guy. About that: You are so adrenalized at this point you could screw up on points one through eight faster than the blink of an eye. Some will try and get you to make a statement now. Know that the police are not required to make a statement on an officer-involved shooting for seventy-two hours. This is to ensure that they have had at least one sleep cycle and because details will be fuzzy immediately after a traumatic event. Adrenaline will tell you to make your statement now. Resist this impulse. Wait until you can clearly remember the event so you get the important facts into your taped statement.[43] The problem here is that your first babbled account is often not an accurate recounting of what happened. If you go on record with incorrect details and try to change them later it spells sudden death. You are viewed as a liar—and once a liar, always a liar.

---

43 In the course of a traumatic event confabulation often happens. This is when you remember points A and C in an event but cannot remember B (or how you got to C). When this happens, your brain tends to "fill in the gaps" with information that seems reasonable. A tricky prosecutor will ask you 'reasonable sounding questions (that he knows the answer to) then nail you with video that says you're lying. For example, our old friend adrenal distortion. Your statement said five feet video shows fifteen.

They will ask questions that minimize your attacker's actions. A tactic we see often is a prosecutor asking how you could shoot an attacker who "only had a knife." In that case you'll need to explain the Tueller Principle (explained in the next chapter). Not only that, but you knew this information before you acted in self-defense against an attacker with a knife that would make Crocodile Dundee gulp in disbelief. (This is why documenting your training is important.) Now you can educate the jury just like you were educated.

Your attorney has to know to ask the questions the opposing counsel didn't. If your attorney is present during questioning he can also force the interviewing officer to allow you to introduce exculpatory evidence (evidence that helps your case) Or, if you answer without your attorney present he can argue how the officer didn't fully investigate (deliberately didn't ask certain questions before charging you).

Lawyers typically don't think in terms of self-defense. They consider things in terms of legal tactics. Most of their clients are guilty so much of their work is not about acquittal but damage control. That's done outside the courtroom. In the courtroom, the acquittal of 'the guilty' is done by undermining the state's case. However, the strategy necessary to defend an affirmative defense (such as SD) is different from trying to get someone off. (Remember in a self-defense situation, you have already admitted to the elements of a crime.) As you explain the situation, your lawyer is translating what you say into legal strategies.

Totality of circumstance versus nitpicking details. Repeating what Massad Ayoob says about totality of circumstances: *The totality of the circumstances suggests that there is no single factor to base a use of force decision on meaning that you must take into consideration all the facts and context to conclude from the whole picture that you acted appropriately.* When you say you saw something and it meant __________, the prosecutor will begin to nitpick. That's where totality of circumstances comes in, it is an anti-nitpick strategy. ("In another context ______ could mean that, in these circumstances it means...")

Given these thirteen points do you now understand why defending a self-defense claim can be so difficult? You must first recognize a threat, then act appropriately, and also explain any use of force to everyone involved with the criminal system. And remember the civil side of this? Everyone wants their meal. Knowing this kind of stuff puts them on a diet.

If you want to stay out of prison fear of getting hurt isn't the standard to determine how much force you need. Fear typically leads to excessive force. Yes you do what you need to do to stay safe, but the tricky part is to know why what you used was the appropriate level for the circumstances.

Use of Force and Scaling Force

Marc explains self-defense as a large square taped to the floor. Imagine standing in the middle of it. You have the right to act within those boundaries to keep yourself safe. But you don't get to decide where those are. The square is the lowest level of force necessary and for it to be self-defense your actions must stay inside that square. Cross those lines (participation, excessive force, not stopping in time, and similar reactions) and what you did was no longer self-defense. A higher level of force puts you on a large table inside that square. Next level is a coffee table. Then a chair. Finally lethal force is you standing on a box on that chair.

Welcome to the wonderful world of scaling force. Starting with it's height and breadth. The higher the force level, the more narrow the restrictions. Yes you can use a necessary level of force to protect yourself, however, circumstances allowing for the higher levels are limited and more dangerous.

Going back to the stacked idea, imagine cops and prosecutors shaking the tables and kicking the legs. At the same time imagine you jumping up and down and dancing around. Are you doing it on the floor or higher up? Both have a lot to do with how much it will hurt if you fall.

Another reason this stacking model works is when the idea of 'winning' causes you to jump levels. This includes skipping levels into excessive force. Did you do what you had to or did you go too high? We won't go into it, but you really should research force levels and scaling for the circumstances. It's entirely different than 'winning.' Here are a few points to look into: How is a punch viewed in your state? A punch is higher up the use of force scale than you might think. You automatically jump levels if you have something in your hand when you hit someone. If you choose to carry a strike enhancer or other type of 'self-defense item' you've already jumped from the level of simple battery to aggravated battery. What's scary is how many people unwittingly hit someone like this. You're holding a drink, someone swings, and you hit back. Viola! aggravated assault.

At the same time, one of the greatest physical dangers to you is when someone uses a higher level of force and *you* respond with an insufficient amount of force. Another complication is the ability to change levels (up or down) as circumstance change *in the middle* of an incident. Scaling force takes a whole lot more than a soundbite answer.

Strong emotions whether anger or fear are reasons most people cross these boundaries, jump levels or overbalance. It's easy to blow it when you're emotional. That's why the 'standing on smaller and higher platforms' is a useful image. It's easy to understand how simple it is to make mistakes and fall.

Perhaps the biggest benefit of this stacking model is it helps you understand why we're taking a top-down approach instead of going from the ground up. We start at lethal force and work back from there.

That isn't how it's usually presented, but we have our reasons. Knowing when you *can't* legally use lethal force immediately takes that option *off the table* for situations that don't justify it—and *you know it.* (We've given you the tools to figure out why that's important.) This lets you focus on options that still work and are more appropriate for the circumstances and the threat level. Presenting it this way makes for faster (and more reliable) decision-making processes about how much force you need.

When is it appropriate to act in self-defense? You are allowed to react to the *immediate* level of danger the person poses to your body. If someone attempts (or is about to try) to cause you harm that's an immediate threat. Here's something many people—especially those who are scared and adrenalized—screw up. An immediate threat consists of what is *actually happening* not what you're afraid *might occur*. For example, you can't kick him when he's down because you're afraid he *might* get up and attack again. That's not an immediate threat. He has to be lunging at you from the ground (and yes that's as difficult as it sounds).

The next thing we would like you to know requires us to get legally argley-bargley. Going back to Colorado Revised Statutes 18-1-704, Use of Physical Force in Defense of a Person:

> (Part 1) Use of Physical Force in defense of a person (1) Except as provided in subsections (2) and (3) of this section, a person is justified in using physical force upon another person in order to defend himself or a third person from what he reasonably believes to be the use or imminent use of unlawful physical force by that other person, and he may use a degree of force which he reasonably believes to be necessary for that purpose.

That means: You *may* use the amount of force necessary to stop the threat. The caveat is you've made an informed assessment about the danger you face. That said, you damn well better *know* exactly how much force you need in the circumstance—and be able to explain it. That's where most people don't just fall down, they high dive into an empty pool. You *cannot* rely on the danger you face being obvious to everyone else. You have to be able to explain the danger you were in *at the time* and how you knew it wasn't just your imagination (pre-existing knowledge).

Take for example someone who tries to grab a cop's gun in a scuffle. This is a big fear for police and *it's well founded*. While there's disagreement over exact numbers when control of the officer's gun is gained by an adversary, there's about a 90 percent chance of the officer being shot. So if someone deliberately goes for a cop's gun—that's it. The officer will shoot that person. This is no longer about making an arrest, it's morphed into officer survival, and *he knows it.* The officer has pre-existing knowledge of what would happen if the person gets his gun and the person 'acts in a manner consistent with 'cop killers.' Because he knows this—and can articulate it—unless there's something extraordinary about the incident, the officer will be cleared. This is not a case of cops 'getting away with murder;' police officers know how dangerous this is and how to react. They also know how to explain it in court. *That* is what we're trying to get across here.

How do you know what level of force is right for you to employ? Understand 'how do you know...' is a fly-over question. There are important considerations people tend to zoom over:

- You must have a scale of danger and probable outcomes.
- You have to know when it's okay to act.
- You have to know how much you can act.
- It has to be within the time frame you have available.

The first consideration is *information* that exists *independent of you.* These are external standards, information, and categories. That means other people know and accept these circumstances *as* dangerous (e.g., jeopardy). You have to learn this general information and do it *before* it becomes personal. Remember the cop knows why someone getting his gun is bad? He knew that *before* he found himself in such a situation.

Using the stacked self-defense model what actions by an attacker would you file on different levels? Example: If someone lunges at you with a knife in his hand, the level of force it takes to stop that attack—*in time*—is higher than the level of force you would reasonably be able to use on someone who is the same size and about to hit you (bare hands). But what if the person about to hit you outweighs you by seventy-five pounds?

Another example is if someone were to trip you as you walked through a parking lot. Deadly force is not an appropriate response to being tripped. You can't shoot him for standing and laughing at you because any danger has passed. Unless he *then* tries to stomp you (the shod human foot against a downed person is considered a lethal force instrument in certain states) or tries for a ground-and-pound on concrete *that's* immediate danger. The trip created the conditions, but the danger lies in the additional elements. See how quickly details can change and *with them* how the 'right answer' changes too? This harkens back to high-speed problem solving and being able to think on the fly.

External standards are an introduction to the *difference* between fear and danger. The fact there is a difference is news to people (namely those who haven't dealt with actual danger). Fear is an *emotion.* It's internal. Yes it's fueled by adrenaline, but it's not the same thing. You can wallow in fear, dance around it, hyperfocus on it, act out of it (usually overdoing it), but at the end of the day it's both subjective and not that important.[44]

44 Everything we've said in that paragraph also applies if you replace the word "fear" with "anger."

Danger is external. It also is physical.

Actions in a dangerous situation show more of a 'get-it-done' mentality. There is no time to decide how you feel about it. (A common reason for the dreaded freeze.) Danger has to be the first thing addressed. If you are truly in danger there is the element of fear, but it is a low priority. When you are in danger, you have bigger problems to deal with than your 'feelz.'

You do *not* want to base your decisions on fear. It sounds like we're repeating ourselves, but this is a subtle and important distinction. Fear-based decisions are usually bad ones. Think about the emotional decisions you've made in your lifetime. How many of those came back to bite you in the butt? It's normal for fear to be present. Acknowledge it and move on to handle the danger of the situation.

It's hard to make an appropriate use of force decision—physically and legally—when you act exclusively on emotions. This is another reason the soundbite of "I was in fear for my life" is not all that it's cracked up to be. Being "in fear" *isn't* enough. Acting from fear means you haven't just moved out of the boundaries of self-defense, you climbed up and dove off. Remember Liam Jackson talking with the prosecutor? Prosecutors have heard the fear defense before and know how to blow it out of the water. Remember the courts *don't care about your feelings*. They do care if you acted appropriately and if you can justify it.

The second and third considerations mean you have to know *when* it's okay to act and *how* much force to use. The 'okay to act' part has three distinct meanings. It's also where the two authors have different approaches. We're going to give you both to think about. (We'll include Jeff Meek's opinion, too. Remember he's also a firearms instructor.)

Jenna's take: My business—as a firearms instructor—is to teach people about the use of lethal force because a gun is per se a 'deadly weapon.' Using one is always deadly force. As Mas Ayoob says, "You can't deliver a boo-boo with a firearm." I would be remiss if I did not teach *when* to use such force. I pass on to my students what I learned: Deadly force is authorized when there is *an immediate and otherwise unavoidable danger of death or grave bodily harm to the innocent.* This is the single best description I have heard for the time when you are justified to use deadly force. This description cuts to the chase of all the elements that *must be* present in order for you to be authorized for such a level of force. If you have time to run away, then I submit that you are not in immediate danger of anything and getting the heck out of there should be your answer.

The decision to use the highest level of force is not something you do when you are facing the threat—by then it's too late. Decisions to use deadly force and knowing the circumstances where this applies need to have been thought through before you find yourself in trouble. By telling you when you are authorized to use deadly force, I give you permission to act if all the necessary elements are present. Your life is worth defending. Not because of who you are to other people, but because you are you. But even with that permission, you need to take a long look in the mirror and decide if you are able to potentially take the life of another if it means saving yourself. If the answer is no, you need tools other than a gun in your toolbox.

Jeff's take: It's true that when you face an attacker, you make instantaneous decisions about deadly force. But if you don't have a firm understanding of your own threat assessment model beforehand, as well as having already made the decision that "yes, there are indeed circumstances in which I will use deadly force," you have *decided not to act.* A better person than I once said, "Not to speak is to speak, not to act is to act." Kicking the can down the road in hopes that deadly force decisions will come naturally when the time comes is a decision—you've decided that you *will not* use deadly force. Make that decision now. Right now. Stop reading and say out loud, "My life is worth defending. I will take the life of another human being if necessary."

Now we can focus on the responsibility that comes with the decision you just made. We can learn how to do that, legally and safely. We can discuss things like good belts and holsters; the Tueller Principle; changing the script; where to aim; and how to interact with responding or investigating officers. Not before. Without having made that decision, our discussion should center around what nice things your kids should say about you at your funeral or who will inherit your shoe collection.

Marc's take: There is a strong bias in this culture against violence—to the point of operant conditioning. We're told nice people aren't violent. Since you're a nice person you're likely to wait too long before you react. This delay poses a bit of a problem. Your self-defense training won't help if you're already being beaten down before you can use it.

Let's take a closer look at this conditioning, where it works and where it doesn't. It's true that most situations are better resolved through nonviolent means. If possible you *should* attempt to use those with your fellow citizens. That's where the anti-violence conditioning works.

On the other hand there are times and places—while rare—when using force is the best answer. And believe it or not it's also the *most reasonable* option. It is unreasonable for you to be expected to die because a third party believes violence is *wrong* and thinks you *'should have tried to* ______ instead. We have to ask, "Did _______ have a reasonable chance of success given the circumstances?" While usually the circumstances are such that a nonviolent solution will work, sometimes that's *off* the table.

The challenging part is knowing how to determine this. This so you can first, give yourself permission and second, react in time. That permission is easier if you have pre-existing knowledge about extreme circumstances, levels of danger, and the probable outcome of not acting. Under those circumstances permission isn't the challenge; the challenge is to decide how much force you'll need and using it. When you need to focus on these decisions, you can't afford to trip over your social conditioning.

Each of these perspectives are valid and offer important considerations. It's well worth taking the time to think each over. There's no right or wrong answer, but they'll help you understand why things aren't as simple or as cut and dried as you previously thought.

We'd also like to toss in something that has a lot to do with 'when to and when not to act.' You need to understand what your rights are depending on *where you are*. We won't go into it, but it has a quite a bit to do with property lines. Pay special attention if you leave your own property. That's not only what blew up our friend Tyler's claim of self-defense (in the first story), but it's a real common attack strategy by prosecutors. (Just ask Raul Rodriguez.) And like the Tyler story, the cops *will* ask.

The *fourth* consideration is available time.

We're going to look at this multifaceted subject from a different angle. If you have ever watched a Hollywood action movie, you have a distorted understanding of time when it comes to violence. The bigger problem is, *so does the jury.*

Going to the extreme of lethal force how fast do you expect a bullet to take effect? Do you expect it to be like the movies where you shoot him, and he immediately falls down (or—sillier still—flies back)? It will surprise you, but many people who have been hit by a stray bullet don't even know they've been shot. They keep on walking. The bad news is if someone is charging you, it can take multiple shots before the collective trauma causes him to collapse. In the meantime, he can still potentially close the distance and bury a knife in your chest. That's known as the "Deadman's Ten" (when someone fatally wounded can still keep attacking anywhere from ten seconds up to two minutes). That's how time in violence really works. Unfortunately the jury will judge your actions by the Hollywood bias of time—and the prosecutor will encourage that. (Your side must explain that's *not* how things work.)

Now that you know about the Deadman's Ten, you'll want to have a working plan if an attacker reaches you—instead of just pulling the trigger again. Will you need to pull it again? Probably. But you'll need to do something else to keep from dying. (That meat cleaver he's swinging at your head isn't going to stop itself.)

In the courtroom, the prosecution's pet doctor will testify that *any* of the three gunshot wounds would be fatal. The jury has seen bad guys on TV stopped immediately with only one shot. On the other hand, TV murderers shoot people multiple times. You shot him three times. Between that, the prosecutor, and the media going on about the family left behind—guess what the jury is thinking you did?

But what about less than lethal force? If getting shot takes that long to take effect how long will it take your punch? Very seldom does one punch work to stop someone committed to attacking you. So we're back to hitting more. The prosecutor will sell *this* as you were fighting.

There's another time consideration here. The length of time it takes for your actions to take effect versus how *fast* he can damage you. How fast will his actions injure you and render you *incapable* of defending yourself (against further injury)? This isn't standing and trading damage—it's a race to stop him before he does unto you.

For example, take anybody who teaches defense against a knife attack that involves punching the attacker as its main component. That's already floated off into fantasyland. To wound you—*all he has to do is touch you.* Once you start getting cut how long do you have? Do you know how to incapacitate someone with your bare hands inside three seconds or is your answer to punch and kick more? This is the part the prosecutor wants *the jury* to overlook, at the same time he says that *you* overreacted to the danger posed by the other person.

You are legally justified in defending yourself when someone is *in the act* of trying to hurt you. When you approach this from the perspective of available time, it helps you understand the problem better.

Here's another question about time: Do you realistically have time to get away? This is a double-edged sword. *One* edge—if someone charges you he can run faster forward than you can *backward*. By back-pedaling, you might get one or two steps before he plows into you. Still on that same edge—how much ground can he cover in the time it would take you to turn and step? Now he T-bones you. Then there's the time it takes you to get up to speed to escape.

The *other* edge of the sword—did you have time to retreat, but instead chose to 'dig in,' regardless if it was to fight or a freeze? By the time you start moving again is it too late?

Another available time issue is how long will it take to get through a locked door to safety? This is one more subject where doing the Tueller Drill is going to change what you think you know. How long does it take you to unlock a door, get through it, and lock it again to keep him out? Time yourself and see how long it takes. Then test to see how much ground someone can cover. And is it really safety? Many women have attempted to flee to the perceived safety of their cars—forgetting they have to start them, put them in gear, pull out or back out. Even if she manages to get in the car window is easily busted out.

What about creating distance? Remember *distance equals time*. Have you looked into how taking a few steps can buy yourself time to mentally shift gears and prepare for what you have to do? If a guy waving a club charges you so fast standing there you're out of options, taking a few steps gives you more time—and by extension, more options. Also if you duck out of the way of an attack where is it written that you have to stay and fight? People don't often see that the same action that avoids an attack gives them a straight shot to the door. Extra points for if you try to get out of the situation.

In case you missed the elephant in the room, time also is *immediate danger.* If you were to get into a verbal tiff with someone and he says something like, "Now you've done it, I am going home to get my gun, come back and shoot you. Just give me an hour because traffic is terrible this time of day." Are you in immediate danger? No of course not but you might be in an hour (depending on traffic). So this would be a good time to get out of there and not wait around to find out how much traffic there really is.

What we've said here is not the end all and be all of learning how to scale the force you have to use, but to introduce you to why incorporating the concept into your training is important. Unfortunately, most training treats this whole subject as a fly-over issue.

To help you get started, there are two introductory books by Rory Miller, *Scaling Force* and *Force Decisions: A Citizen's Guide to Understanding How Police Determine Appropriate Use of Force.* Instead of listening to a grand master of an ancient warrior art or your gunfighting goo-roo, you might want start with what really works—especially in the context of defending yourself in court.

We're going to close this chapter with an idea of how this works in real life. A newer model of police scaling and use of scaling looks like this:

- Presence (their presence deters crime)
- Verbal (orders)
- Empty hands (control hold, kicks, punches, joint manipulation, etc.)
- Less than lethal (tasers or pepper spray)
- Lethal (shooting)

Straight from Capt. Jon Lupo (who reviewed this book): *Many police agencies have adopted "use of force" models that more strongly emphasize the need to be able to de-escalate the level of force during a given situation, as well as escalate. These agencies now frequently refer to a "force continuum" or "quantum of force" model, intending to address the fluid, changeable nature of situations where it is necessary for a law enforcement officer to adjust his or her use of force as circumstances change.*

First, we just gave you three different models from *inside* a profession. Those models represent changes in the application, equipment, legal challenges, and education about a subject. Complex problems are so fluid not only do cops have to adapt—*so do you.*

Second, these levels correlate with the chances of injury (not pain, injury) that the officers and suspects are likely to undergo. In plain English, that means how likely is someone to get hurt or killed?

These same challenges apply to you when it comes to scaling force. You can't come up with the right answer if you don't understand the problem. The nature of the problem should make more sense now.

'21 Foot Rule,
Shut Up and Lawyer Up,
I'd rather be judged by twelve than carried by six,'
and other noise that makes us twitch.

Debunking Soundbites

By now we hope we've inoculated you against many of the soundbites and clichés that run rampant in the self-defense world. In many ways now knowing what you do will make you like the only person in a leper colony who doesn't have leprosy. The problem with that is how often those with the disease will see that as something's wrong with you.[45]

For example, people who maintain *always* 'shut up and lawyer up' will tell you you're wrong about talking to the cops. When it comes to small incidents their position is unrealistic—and expensive. It's better to learn how to make statements to cops for small offenses. It's cheaper, too. This is especially important because—if the other guy is a good liar—the police will arrest you because all they have to go on is the other's lies. Many cases are—*he said and he said*. The person with a better statement or who is first to get on record will have his name put on the victim line on the police report; the other is written up as the perpetrator. If only one side does any talking…

To help you navigate the minefield of soundbite self-defense let's ask a basic question: *Is it a soundbite, a cliché, an aphorism, or a fundamental?*

Here are some eye-opening definitions:

- *Soundbite:* a short extract from a recorded interview chosen for its pungency or appropriateness.
- *Cliché*: a phrase or opinion that is overused and betrays a lack of original thought.

45 This is a good news and bad news situation. The good news is that you are now more prepared to handle what violence may come your way. The bad news is that being part of a small minority (who understand this), you'll probably get as cranky as we are. Next thing you know you'll be yelling at kids to get off your lawn.

- *Aphorism*: a pithy observation that contains a general truth, such as "if it ain't broke don't fix it."
- *Fundamental:* (n)—a central or primary rule or principle on which something is based or arises from.

What you want in any short summation are the last two, *not* the first two. This is the difference between a soundbite statement (such as "I'd rather be judged by twelve than carried by six") and something that is actually useful information (e.g., Don't run from danger run toward safety). Being able to tell the difference is a useful skill.

What we're about to give you is an example of a simplistic—and wrong—soundbite versus something that has practical application to understanding threats, your ability to react in time, and how to explain your actions to others (attorney, jury, etc.). We're talking about the twenty-one-foot principle.

Wait. Principle? I thought it was the "21 Foot Rule."

For those not familiar with this bit of soundbite stupidity, it is often presented as "if someone is within twenty-one feet, I can shoot them." Then they go on about how this defense strategy is scientifically proved and a police policy. *This couldn't be farther from the truth.*

So you know, it's not even the 21 Foot Principle, it's called the "Tueller Principle." Let's look at why it's both so much more and important.

Dennis Tueller (a trainer and sergeant with the Salt Lake City Police Department at the time) published an article titled, *How Close is Too Close* in the March 1983 issue of SWAT Magazine.[46] In a nutshell: Police had been injured. They also faced public outrage and bad press about shootings where the assailants "only had a knife." The article detailed Tueller's research on officer injury and policy. At the time a standard for officers was to draw their gun from an open carry holster and fire two shots at a target seven yards away (twenty-one feet). The *average* time for this was 1.5 seconds. Tueller then looked at the distance an assailant with a 'contact weapon' could cover and use the weapon in that same 1.5 seconds. The answer coincidentally was—on average—twenty-one feet.

46 https://bit.ly/1uWMHRA

Some people could cover *much more*. When the attacker reached the officer, they exchanged damage. The whole subject turned out to be more complex and required further research. The drill had a major influence on departmental policies about when officers can draw their guns and—in court—why 'shooting someone charging an officer *before* reaching the officer' was considered a reasonable response. And Dennis Tueller was pretty clear about it being a *principle* and not a rule.[47] Yet in the soundbite self-defense world, it's intoned as "The 21 Foot Rule" by wannabe gunfighters.

Oh look, Jenna feels another rant coming on. *One of the dumbest things I hear in the self-defense world is "if someone is within twenty-one feet of me I'll just shoot them." (True story, we hear it all the time). Jeff once responded to such a comment with how fun dinner parties at this guy's house must be. The response was, "Well, that's not what I meant." Well, that's what you said. If a prosecutor can lay his hands on that kind of comment, he'll sell it as premeditation. It won't be a hard sell. When you say stuff like that it sounds like you were just itchin' to shoot someone. You'd be better served to understand the actual principle and how it applies rather than just rattling off something to impress people on the Internet. It's even worse if you actually think that spouting '21 Foot Rule' gives you the same license to shoot someone as saying 'I was in fear for my life.'*

The Tueller Drill is a great tool to help you understand what's involved in an actual attack. Both authors have run versions (with blue guns for safety) and can attest to how eye-opening it is for people. Under stress you find a plethora of problems you didn't even dream about much less have viable solutions for...

Things like the difficulty of drawing a gun from *concealment* in time when someone charges you. (This makes it easy to bungle the draw, causing it to take more time to get your gun into the fight.) Do the drill yourself, you'll find all kinds of things to look into like how the length of time to 'make the decision to act' decreases as you do more repetitions. (On the first run through, we've seen an attacker cover fifteen feet before the good guy even started to move—and that's knowing he was about to be attacked.) Another is how hard it is to move off line while drawing and under pressure. (The hard part isn't physical, it's overcoming mental and emotional 'restrictions.') How if you can move you also have to work on the

---

47 ACLDN video Additional Considerations When Using Deadly Force: Interviews with Advisory Board Members by Marty Hayes, J.D.

timing so your attacker doesn't simply change his course. Then there are the unexpected benefits of moving at the right time and some really fascinating results—especially how it messes with an attacker's head and what steps he has to take to attack again. It gives you all sorts of extra time. Then there are the things you have to do if an attacker does manage to close the distance. Actions you didn't have to deal with when he was fifteen feet away.

These are some of the items of pre-existing knowledge you *won't have* if you've bought into the '21 Foot Rule' soundbite. Think it's worth looking into? Now how many other soundbites have you heard—especially about using force and talking with the cops?

Addendum: We've had reports that criminals—especially in shall issue states—also know about the '21 Foot Rule,' and exploit it. Criminals know in a shall issue state there are a lot more concealed guns out there, so one hangs back outside this range and makes noise. While your attention is focused on him, his partner sneaks up on you from behind (which makes eyes up, head on a swivel a working strategy in this kind of situation).

Don't fail the personality test
Officer Kasey Keckeisen, founder, Violence Dynamics

Dealing with the Cops

Another soundbite you're probably familiar with is "don't talk to the cops." You hear it from all kinds of dudes on the Internet and even from criminal defense attorneys. We want to give you more details so you can make an informed decision on what to say especially at the scene *if* you acted in self-defense.

But before you worry about what to say to the police let's address not getting yourself shot when they roll up. Starting with some basics:

Step one: It doesn't matter how emotional, adrenalized, or self-righteous you are *you do not have the right* to refuse a lawful order from an officer in the execution of his duties.

If you don't think it's lawful, remember these simple standards:

- Not here.
- Not now.
- Not you.

Save it for court. Don't disobey or try to argue for your rights then and there. The only thing you'll do is make a bad situation worse (usually by breaking other laws). This is a never-forget rule because refusal to comply authorizes the officer to use force.

Step two: How long do you think a call from dispatch lasts? A lot of that time is spent giving the officers the address, the threat level (code), and the nature of the call. This information has been interpreted and labeled by the dispatcher (e.g., a domestic disturbance). Putting that in plain English, it means the patrol officer shows up with minimal—maybe even incorrect—information. That's with a radio call. If they were driving by and saw violence, they know even less. So now might be a good time to learn how to *not* get shot or beaten by the police when they arrive.

For ease of explanation let's take this to the level of a self-defense shooting. Knowing that they're responding to a shooting, it's understandable the officers will be concerned about a person with a gun. Once they get to the scene, they have no clear idea of what is going on or who is the good guy and who is the bad guy. This can be especially confusing if you—the good guy—still have a gun in your hand when they arrive on the scene.[48]

The officers' first priority is to *secure the scene*. That means the first thing on their to-do list isn't your rights or who did what. It's to take control of the situation, so they can *safely* start to sort things out. This is why the first thing you need to know—and never forget—is when the cops roll up *the situation has changed.* There's now a five hundred- pound gorilla in the room, and it's dictating the rules for the moment. Like we said earlier, "Drop the gun" means drop the gun—*now*!

Speaking of now, remember Mr. Adrenaline is still there and *if you let him dictate your actions,* you're going to fail the personality test. *Only* take the actions the officers tell you to do. Take for example—talking. Odds are the first thing he's going to tell you is step back and wait. Do it. Step back, shut up, and wait for one of them to come talk to you. Why? Police have lots of experience with fighters flying at each other even after they've arrived. (Remember Mr. Adrenaline?) One of the signs of things heading this way is when people demand to be heard first—usually by refusing to step back and wait their turn. You will get your chance to talk to the officer, but if you act like a demanding child before the situation is controlled you're part of the reason the situation isn't considered contained.

Step Three: When they roll up, it sends a good message if they see you shift gears. For example, you see them and step back without being ordered to. (It also helps to show your open hands… they notice nice little gestures like that.) Stepping away and waiting is a type of nonverbal communication akin to rolling down the window and keeping your hands in plain sight when pulled over at a traffic stop.[49] This sends the message you know the situation is

---

48 It's worth mentioning if you are the one to call 911 tell them that you are the victim and give dispatch a physical description of yourself. Leave out things like hats and glasses that can be removed or lost, so there is no confusion. Giving them a description of your clothing shirt pants, and jacket (and don't change those), height/ weight and any other distinguishing characteristics are good. Don't bother getting to creative or informative as the call will be admissible evidence.

49 As opposed to leaning over, rooting through your glove compartment, swearing about being pulled over, and making comments about his mother.

serious, you know his concerns, you're not interested in being a problem, and you'll cooperate with their doing their job. This might be easier said than done under the effects of adrenaline so it is important to practice shifting from acting to communicating ahead of time.

One of the first things we did was introduce you to thinking of a self-defense incident as a three-part process (the pre-, the physical, and the aftermath). Hopefully you started to shift into aftermath thinking before the police arrive, but when they roll up that's the latest you want to do it. Your physical part is done. Now you get to stand aside and let the cops go to work. You have to help them do their job, however. Part of that is being patient and following their orders. Not only will this keep you from getting shot or tased, but it gives you time to mentally review what happened, rough out your strategy, and compose yourself. It's helpful if you are calm and cooperative—and the other guy isn't.

Don't freak out if the officers want to put you in handcuffs immediately upon their arrival. If the situation involved a high level of violence, *it's going to happen*. You do not suddenly lose the ability talk when you are handcuffed (or sitting on the curb). Nor does it automatically mean you are under arrest—which brings us to talking with the police.

What we're about to say may sound contradictory to what we said earlier when it comes to the police. We need to tell you that there are good cops, bad cops, mediocre cops, and cops who have to follow orders. You don't know what you're going to get, so cover all your bases.

Why is knowing that there are different types of cops and how they work important? After violence occurs and the police show up, it's too much to try to come up with a good strategy and learn how things work at the same time. Like everything else about this subject, it's time to act on *what you already know*. That means you've done your homework beforehand.

We've discussed the problems with soundbites, but now it's time to talk about how to avoid the pitfalls of talking to the cops. Remember the police are professionals so *don't* underestimate them and don't assume they're out to get you. That's a bigger topic—and challenge—than you know.

There are some people who start with the attitude that all cops are out to get them. They usually turn this into a self-fulfilling prophecy via their behavior. Most people's thinking about the police start at "I acted in self-defense" and "when the cops show up they'll immediately recognize I'm the good guy." That's *not* a good way to look at it. Stepping back, let's get a bigger picture.

Capt. Jon Lupo, a thirty-one-year veteran of the New York State Police, once explained[50] it to Marc this way: *Police officers are safety officers. One of our fundamental roles is to preserve safety- ours, yours, the victim's, and the suspect's (where applicable). When we arrive whether it's a crime scene, an accident scene, or something else in addition to keeping everyone safe, we also have to investigate what happened. Using an extreme example, let's say we roll up and find a person deceased. Did they die of natural causes? Perhaps commit suicide? Die in a car crash or an industrial accident? Were they killed by another person? It's our responsibility to figure that out. If we have reason to believe a crime was committed, we begin investigating the circumstances of that crime and who did it in order to help build a case for the prosecutor.*

Notice that the cops don't start out assuming you've done wrong. That can happen during the process—especially if they find out you crossed the line from self-defense or they catch you in a lie. Your behavior could influence that change—even if you did act within the boundaries of self-defense. And if you didn't act right to begin with if there is any further misbehavior with the cops, you'll really screw the pooch.

Earlier we said the cops are professionals. They have training, tricks, procedures, and goals you don't even know about. For example, did you know during a traffic stop when the cop asks you a question while you're looking for your proof of insurance it's a test to see if you're drunk? Drunks can't multitask. If you fail you've given him probable cause to proceed investigating if you're driving while drunk.

That's just one of the *professional moves* cops have. Learn about the most common elements they look for. (This is when having law enforcement instructors and friends is golden.) While you're not going to 'beat a professional' at his own game, you can avoid stumbling into common pitfalls. Be especially aware of 'innocent' questions about scaling force. For example, the question, "Did you hit him?"

That's part of a story about the last time Marc had a gun pointed at him by a cop. In the officer's defense, Marc was kneeling

---

50 That's cop talk for pinning Marc's ears back.

on someone's head... late one night... in the middle of the sidewalk... while his co-worker sat on the guy's legs. Being ordered to get off said gentleman's head by the gunslinger, Marc held up his hands and declared, "I will cooperate, but you need to know he's on the fight. If I let him up, he's going to attack us again."[51] No points were gained by the officer when he replied he was willing to take that chance. Marc and his partner stood up and stepped away. With the arrival of extra officers, Marc and his co-worker ended up talking to the officer, explaining they worked in the building. The drunk had first attacked some customers and then them when they intervened. The officer asked, "Did you hit him?" (Higher on the force scale.) "No, sir. I used a prescribed takedown to stop him from attacking my partner." (Takedowns are a soft hands technique by police standards.)

Around this time, the quarrelsome drunk referred to a female officer by a part of her anatomy. Marc and his co-worker were told they could leave. As they went back inside, the drunk had new friends kneeling on his head (and the female officer was really working that knee). Total time from looking down the barrel of a cop's gun to walking away—under five minutes. That's how important it is to be able to talk to the cops and make statements.

Something else you need to know is people lie to the cops all the time. One of the most important things you have to do is convince him you aren't one of them. In fact, lying is the fastest way to fail the personality test with a police officer. Another cop trick? When the lights go on, it's damned near instinctive to look down at the speedometer. (Unless you saw him earlier and tried to slow down.) So when the cop asks, "Do you know why I pulled you over?" or "Do you know how fast you're going?" He's either looking for an admission of guilt (that you were speeding) *or a lie.* ("No, officer, I don't.")

Do yourself a favor and *do not* start your interaction with cops by lying or being hostile, angry, or demanding. That behavior sets a negative tone from which you will probably never recover—unless the other person proves himself to be a bigger jerk.[52] Another Keckiesen quote is, *I've never had anyone talk themselves out of being arrested, but a lot of people have talked themselves into being arrested*"

---

51 Knowing what you know now, what important information was immediately conveyed to the police in just three sentences?

52 This includes you going off on Libertarian rants, your rights, and challenges about "Am I being detained?"

That brings us to the next point of *not assuming the cops are out to get you.* People who are deeply into the 'victim narrative' often have this attitude. As do people who think they're too good to deal with the cops. People are going to ascribe negative reactions by the police to _______ (whatever) when 98 percent of the time the cop's attitude boils down *to their behavior.* This especially means the hostility toward cops for doing their job. And right now, the cop's job *is you*. Your job is to deal with that as an adult.

- Yes, there are cops who are assholes and on power trips.
- Get over it. You have bigger problems you need to deal with.
- They are the ones with the pen.
- Even so, they must operate within the limits of the process.

The reality is about 90 percent of all the 'Little Bo Peep' stories about evil, power trippin' cops come from people whose behavior wasn't all that sweet and innocent. In fact they were uncooperative and insulting, if not hostile. Don't forget police are humans too, and nobody likes to be lied to, looked down on, or insulted.

Your little duck feelings and his behavior are really minor problems. There's something much bigger going on. The presence of the cops is akin to a giant machine that has been started and is warming up. If it is put in gear, someone is going to get chewed up. (You don't want it to be you). There is a trickle-down effect when it comes to officers' doing their jobs. It's not always that the cops are out to get you. They are following orders f*rom higher up* the chain. If they are told they need to make an arrest they will—regardless of what they personally think.

There are some things you need to know.

Starting with once an arrest is made *that machine is on the clock*. They won't arrest until they think they have enough evidence for the district attorney (DA) to prosecute and win. That's one of the differences between a professional and you, he's working with standards *you don't know*—usually because your self-defense instructor never mentioned how important they are to keeping you out of prison.

The decision—and by extension order—to arrest often comes from the investigator, the senior officer present, or from the DA's office (the cops called them and relayed information). This often means that the order to arrest comes from someone *not even present*.

That decision won't happen until they think they have enough evidence to win the case. This goes all the way back to the second chapter. It costs the state money to arrest and prosecute. If they don't think they have enough evidence to get a conviction, they're not going to arrest. The investigating officers are trying to get it.

Moreover typically the person who 'won' is the primary aggressor. That doesn't mean the other person isn't just as much of a participant. In the old days (and with lower levels of injury) it was assumed the situation boiled down to Jerk Number One and Jerk Number Two. Back then the cops could say "Go home or I'll arrest both of you." These days, not so much. Basically it has to do with police departments getting sued if they don't arrest and something happens later. These days it's safer for departments to take the approach of "someone has to go to jail."

Make sure it's the other guy. By agreeing to make a statement—even if it's later—it works in your favor. That's a much, much bigger subject than we want to go into. But we can give you some simple advice.

1. You're going to have to come up with truths that make you look good *faster* than he can come up with lies to make you look bad. (Again using the knee on the head story, Marc's story was consistent, had evidence to back it up, and was delivered in a polite and professional manner. The drunk, not so much).

2. Use the chance to embed preexisting knowledge into your statement. For example: "He moved into attack range" or "I use _____ (insert threat assessment model here) and using that system he..." These kinds of statements make it harder to prosecute you because it shows that you knew *why* what that person was doing was dangerous to you.

3. Also, know an arrest might not be made at the scene. It could be that more evidence comes to light after the initial encounter and then the arrest is made. Being handcuffed doesn't mean you're arrested, you can make a statement at the station. If you're going to claim self-defense you might even have to sit in a cell for a while.

Once again though we want to stress, the higher the use of force, the more important to have your attorney present. That's because the more pressure there is coming from above to arrest you.

We've talked about how to deal with responding officers and how your behavior can help or hurt your case. We did not tell you what to say to the responding officers. Just a note on this, we caution against reciting or reading a script. But what we will tell you is how you talk to the cops has a lot to do with how the report will be written up. This is important because the report is what the DA will base his decision to prosecute or not on.

How to deal with cops is something you should have worked on ahead of time, please look into this and find a solution that works for you, as there are no soundbite or one size fits all answers.

Tyler Story, Ten

Tyler's dad is in bad shape and over the years his health problems have gotten worse. Tyler moved back in with Dad to help out. Dad has never been afraid of confrontation, but over the last few months, his behavior has become more hostile and aggressive. He's also become more erratic and forgetful. Over the last two weeks Dad's been having fits of explosive rage over small things and has become paranoid. They've seen the doctor and tests were scheduled for next week.

Coming home from work one day, Tyler is confronted by Dad about something missing from the garage, and he blames Tyler for taking it. Tyler goes into the garage and finds it right where it's supposed to be. Coming into the kitchen, Tyler finds his dad waiting for him with a chef's knife. Screaming that he knew Tyler took it, Dad attacks. Tyler dodges the initial charge and pulls his concealed carry pistol. Unfortunately his first evasion takes him away from an easy escape route. He screams at Dad to stop, but Dad rushes at him again. Tyler shoots twice. Dad collapses. Tyler holsters his gun, kicks the knife away, pulls out his cell phone, and calls 9-1-1 before trying to stop the bleeding. Dad dies en route to the hospital.

Tyler calls his attorney who agrees to meet him at the station. Cops arrive and start asking questions. Tyler tells them he'll answer but knowing how serious this is he'll do it after he consults with his attorney and only in the presence of his attorney. Tyler is taken to the station where he waits in a cell for a few hours. He takes the time to calm down and review what happened. When his attorney arrives, Tyler consults with her in a private room without cameras. They agree that what he did was self-defense.

Later in a room with video, the detective starts asking questions:

- What happened?
- Why did you think you were in danger?
- How did you know that was dangerous?
- How do you explain shooting a man who only had a knife?
- Could you have used less force?

Tyler tells the whole story. He explains the living circumstances and tells them Dad became more erratic and hostile. He explains tests were scheduled but hadn't happened yet. He said he had just come home, and how he'd tried to placate his father by finding the item—then things exploded. Tyler explains he has a concealed carry permit and that he was in danger because he recognized the presence of ability, opportunity, and jeopardy of the situation. He told the detective how he knew the circumstances of someone acting erratically and increasingly violently toward him, armed with a knife, and closing the distance between them meant he was about to be stabbed. Tyler stated that such an attacker could close and fatally wound him in a matter of seconds. Because it was his father didn't mean the danger wasn't real. He added escape was an unrealistic option because of the way they were positioned after the first attack. Tyler explains how he stopped shooting when Dad collapsed, called 9-1-1, and started trying to save him.

Tyler was able to articulate all of these different things to the detective and was on video telling what happened. His lawyer spotted trick questions and asked the officer to reframe them. Tyler wasn't arrested that night, was released, and told further investigation was pending.

The evidence at the scene matches Tyler's story. Other elements of his story are verified (work hours, doctor's appointments, and other aspects of the case). His articulation goes into the initial report and influences further investigation. The autopsy later reveals that his dad had a brain tumor. The undetected tumor was the cause of his dangerous behavior. Tyler is never charged.

Entirely too many people mistake
confidence for competence.
This makes them extremely vulnerable
to soundbite self-defense instructors

Wide Range of Training Revisited

Now that you have a better understanding of the use of force and what it entails, you can be a bit more selective about the scope of training and the caliber of instructor you choose. Knowing what you do now, you're going to run into a different set of problems.

There are the different levels required to be good at something.

Skill Sets, Skill, Art

Skill Sets: These are core mechanics and abilities many people take for granted. Bad move because skill sets are a lot more complicated than they realize.

Using driving a vehicle to explain the differences, Marc points out there are three main skill sets. They are steering, braking, and accelerating. We'll use braking to explain skill sets. It's not just stomping on the pedal, it's the ability to apply the right amount of pressure to stop the car *at a speed* and *within a set distance* without throwing people through the window. To do this you need to be able to subconsciously calculate speed, distance, and vehicle weight then apply varying amounts of pressure to the brake. (As you decrease speed, you decrease pressure).

The key word is *subconsciously* performing *all that* has been relegated to an unconscious part of your brain. This is so you perform the act without even thinking about it (often mistakenly called 'muscle memory' by the soundbite crowd).

How much of your practice and training time has been focused on the nuts and bolts of your skill sets? This isn't pressure testing yet, it's making sure the components are there. An example of this is Marc's rant about how punching is taught:

- What are the mechanics of a good strike?
- What elements have to be there for effective power transfer?
- What is the range of that move?
- How much time and effort have you spent ingraining these elements and practicing by performing them under stress and against another person's movements?

Most people actually suck at these... then get all whiny and snivel about how 'it didn't work when they tried to use it.' No. It didn't work because they half-assed it and didn't deliver enough force to squish a loaf of bread.

Have you ever thought of punching in such detail? Did your instructor go into the subject in such depth? If not, you're weak in the skillset of punching.

Look for instructors who are big on ingraining skill sets.

Skill: The skill of driving is how you combine the three sets appropriately for the circumstances. Skill is mostly based on extra knowledge, understanding, and context. Inherent in skill is decision making and putting that decision into effect using established guidelines.

For example, you're driving in the slow lane on the freeway and someone comes up the on-ramp and attempts to merge… what do you do?

Skill is the ability to appropriately apply your skill sets in a tense situation. To put this in self-defense terms, effectively blocking in time when an attack comes in. Or being able to execute a technique well enough to end a threat—while someone is trying to hurt you.

Look for instructors who tell you the limits of when and when not to use techniques—especially in regard to larger, stronger opponents.

Art: Transcends the mechanical (skill sets) and situational response (skill). It's where the magic happens.

The art of driving has three facets.

Predictive—That is when you can look at a developing situation that will not manifest for a few moments and adjust a little now so you won't need to do major work later. For example, seeing the other driver on the on-ramp and doing something before he starts to merge so it won't affect you.

*O*pportunity (for effective responses)—Knowing the subject so well you have the ability to see—and act on—openings beginners miss. Because they don't yet have the experience to recognize and respond to what they see much less how to exploit it to their advantage.

*A*ppropriate applications—How do you change your driving when it's warm and dry? Wet and rainy? Foggy and dark? Freeway versus mountain driving? It's all driving, but you have to adjust to conditions.

In the context of self-defense, predictive is extending your radar when entering into a fringe area and spotting the three shady characters spaced out along the wall you have to pass or loitering at the parking lot entrance. Instead of thinking "they're harmless" and walking into their trap, you turn around and go the other way. It might not be sexy and dangerous, but if it keeps you safe it's the ultimate self-defense.

Opportunity is knowing that the mugger stepping into range to pull his weapon means you cannot only jam that draw but introduce him to the concrete at high speed.

Appropriate application starts with recognizing threat levels, scaling force, and building from there.

Look for instructors who strive to help you develop this artistry.

What we have just provided is a way to create an outline for your training. Our hope is that this allows you to get training that covers the often overlooked and most misunderstood topics. Topics that are vital to not only a well-rounded self-defense plan but which will keep you from getting hurt or ending up in the slammer.

A few free-floating points on this subject.

How much pressure testing do you do?

Knowing you have to have skill sets in place before you pressure test makes the results of that testing a whole lot more effective. Otherwise, you'll be flapping around and fumbling. You want to get over fumbling in training and not encounter it for the first time when you're under attack. This is especially true if your self-defense plan includes any type of weapon.

"If it is stupid and it works it isn't stupid" training

When you have the skill sets, skill, and art model under your belt, you're going to start seeing training in a new way. One of the things that suddenly starts making sense are drills that help you develop necessary.

These are often derided by self-appointed masters of the subject as proof of how stupid other people's training is (and by extension how superior theirs is). A good example is what Marc calls the "zombie fist" drill. One person stands in front of another student who extends a fist and shambles forward. Since slow zombies aren't smart, they can't change course. Zombie fist looks stupid, but it's primarily a drill to teach the student to get off line. Yes, that's something you *have to* learn to do when facing another person. (Otherwise, you won't move but will brace for impact.) On a higher level, this drill instills 'faith' that dodging works in a deep part of the brain. Yes, you have to be taught this. Under adrenaline you typically won't do something you don't have faith in. On a still higher level, it teaches the student how to move off line in a balanced and structured manner so he can respond immediately instead of wasting time regaining his balance. After a while the speed of the attacks increases to pressure test these skill sets (yes fast zombies). Another higher level is when the number of attackers change, and you must dodge at least three zombies (slow and fast).

So if it's stupid and it works—it *isn't* stupid.

Fluffer curriculum and fantasy camp

At the same time "if it's stupid…" training is important, there might be a lot of fantasy and fluff added to what you're taught.

A lot of this in the martial arts comes from piling on countless drills, katas, and learning 'new stuff.' The common result is instead of someone becoming good at even one thing, a student grows incompetent at many. You can actually defend yourself by knowing one kata well. Not so much with fifty that you're not even mediocre doing. More and more is piled on instead of ingraining skill sets, skills, and the art.

Fantasy camp is the firearms training equivalent. It's the high-speed, low-drag training that is hella fun to do. This doesn't help you work on skill sets or skills per se, but it helps to open your eyes to applying them in different environments under specialized circumstances. Realistically, how many civilians are going to have to clear a house in the dark? If there is ever a time to call for professional help this is it. YouTube does not constitute training.

That's not training that's *research*. In case you missed it: There is a big difference between training and research. Training is done in person and is led by a qualified professional. This is true of *any* subject that you want to learn about. Some examples include learning first aid, CPR (cardio-pulmonary resuscitation), cooking, or yoga. You take a class or better yet classes to learn a certain set of skills or gain a certain base of knowledge. Then you practice what you learned in class.

Research is all the supporting (or dissenting) information you can learn outside of class. It's reading articles on the topics, watching videos, and more. Doing research is a great way to get a deeper understanding and supplement your knowledge base. It also is a good way to learn both sides of an argument. Real understanding of topics happens when we understand not only our own position but the opposing side as well. But in order to get the most out of your research, you need to some kind of training. Otherwise it's easy to go off into the weeds. Big things will be overlooked. Trivial things will be overly emphasized. And you won't be able to tell the difference until your self-defense tire blows out.

Revisiting skill sets reveals missing fundamentals

All too often people start digging into a subject in the middle when it would be more beneficial to start at the beginning. The beginning is where the fundamentals live. Once you have the fundamentals we can work on the applicable skill sets that encompass those fundamentals, but not before.

Jenna sees this all the time in her training classes. The macho guys who have "been around guns all their lives" and resist the idea that they should take a level one class. It is hard to explain without hurting feelings they will learn something in the beginning class. This is especially true of those who have never taken a formal training class before.

The other side of the coin is where Marc has run into countless black belts who can't punch—literally—to save their lives. Yes, they're fast, but they lack the fundamentals of power generation and delivery. They are, as his wife Dianna says, *Very well trained in bad systems*. Don't you be that guy.

Jack of All Trades (JOAT) mindset versus specialized training

Early on we mentioned the need for a JOAT mindset (basically, knowledge about components other than the physical). With any kind of training there are multiple rabbit holes you can go down in training, but what do you really need? How germane to your needs is a particular subject?

Realistically your needs and wants are often two separate animals when it comes to training. The initial goal is JOAT. That covers the spectrum of what first is needed. Once you have these needs covered, then you can go play down in whatever rabbit holes you want.

Choose an instructor for his or her strong suit and recognize when to branch out

There are some master-class instructors who will help you develop mad Peter Rabbit skills. If you get a chance, we highly recommend taking training from one of them.

But avoid the super Wal-Mart training trap. There's no such thing as one-stop shopping for all your self-defense needs. Once you are comfortable with your level of knowledge about what one instructor can teach you about a topic go investigate another facet of self-defense. Once you've covered the basic spectrum, you can come back to investigate another specific rabbit hole.

When to pick specialized training (the higher the risk, the more training needed)

Are you in a job where there is a high likelihood of violence? Do you have relatives who are violent (including ex's)? Do you live in a crappy neighborhood? Guess what? You're going to need more and better training.

As Marc often says: W*e don't train for if it happens, we prepare for when it happens*. That's an important mindset difference—starting with training for the widest spectrum of violence. This is training for different ranges and different levels of violence. If this doesn't apply to your lifestyle that's fine. Get what you need, then play with other stuff. Maybe a cooking class.

'Only one right way' instructor

Although this problem manifests differently in the martial arts and shooting worlds, it's endemic to both. In the MA world, it's about who has the true style. In shooting, it's over the "right way" to do something.[53] If an instructor takes the "my way or the highway" approach proceed with caution. Not only because the mechanics of what he's teaching might not work for you, but because of the social dynamics that often accompany schools of the 'only true way.'

Do more of the same, but harder and faster

This also could be called "this works if you do it hard enough" training.

This problem goes beyond just "do the mechanics work" and "do you have time and resources." It's also when no matter what the problem is ___________ is the answer. There are other ways to handle things than:

1) do _____ harder and faster
2) the answer to any problem is ______

The example Marc uses is the time he was on an SD instructor forum and someone asked, "How can I carry a gun into the shower with me—in case I'm attacked?" So-called instructors came up with these 'barking moon bat' answers of how to carry while naked. Finally, Marc replied, "Lock your doors and windows. If you feel you have to put a lock on the bathroom door. If you're really paranoid get a motion-activated door alarm and leave your gun on the bathroom counter. But most of all quit pissing people off so bad they'd want to break into your house and kill you!"

If the 'answer' is always the same no matter what the question, you're in the wrong place.

---

53 In the shooting world, this usually starts with the word 'proper.' As in– proper grip. We are all built differently and things that might work for big, tall, muscular guys might not work for … well Jenna stands five foot nothing and has hands the size of a ten-year-old. Do you really think that one "proper" grip will work for all people? (The answer is "no.") The 'right way' for you is what gives you the best results. If you are getting results that work for you then we don't care (as long as you are being safe) how you grip your weapon or how you stand when you shoot. There is one caveat and that is: you need to know how you do what you do. This is key because you will need to replicate this every time you shoot. Do it the same way each time because if you ever have to act in self-defense changing the way you do something mid-incident is a heck of a bad time to get results that you are not expecting.

That secret weapon, which can be stashed in the toolbox of every legally armed citizen, is documented training
Marty Hayes, J.D.

Document your Training

Why on earth should we document our training?

Before we get to the reasons why documenting your training is important, let's talk about *how* to do it. We recommend you keep detailed records of any and all training you have had in the art of self-defense, (in the U.S.) seal copies of them in an envelope and mail them to yourself via certified mail. When the envelope arrives either give it to your attorney, a "trusted other," or put it in some safe place (e.g., a safe or deposit box at a bank).

Items in your dossier can include but are not limited to names, dates, and locations of any training classes and lectures you have attended. Include the name of the instructor(s) and any notes you have from the class. If you rewrite your notes and include a copy of the revised notes (instead of the originals). That is always better since you have had time to digest the material and make more sense of your original notes.

Also, include any research you have done on the topic such as titles of any relevant videos you have watched along with the date you watched them. Titles of books and articles you have read with the dates you read them. These notes should be updated regularly. You decide how often that is (based on your training schedule).

If this becomes court evidence, you will be happy that you have clear, concise notes. If you keep a practice journal for range time or regular classes that is a great thing to put into your dossier.

Important safety tip: Knowing how severe the consequences would be, you made an informed decision to act because you knew the cost of not acting would be worse.

Now that we understand how to document our training let's talk about *why* we do it.

Let's start with the fact that this is a proven strategy. One that police departments use to protect their officers when they've been in use of force incidents. This strategy routinely helps protect and indemnify the departments and officers in both criminal and civil cases. If the time ever comes, you will have a great piece of evidence for your attorney to open in court, which shows the jury that you had a pre-existing base of knowledge and understanding about what is self-defense, how it works, and what's involved. If you were smart enough to get formal training on the legal aftermath of a defensive action—*and have that documented*—then it shows the jury that you not only understood use of force principles, but you also understood how the legal system works ahead of time.

There is a whole lot of suck that comes after using force against another human being, and this is a decision that should never be entered into lightly or as an emotional response. Knowing what we do about use of force and the meat grinder that is the legal system, we find it hard to believe that any citizen would act willy-nilly with force—especially deadly force. And yet that is exactly what happens when people only focus on training for the physical part of SD. Your prior study and documentation to this effect will go a long way to show the jury you acted with the proper care.

This idea of documenting your training might make some old-timers' teeth itch. After all back in the day, the soundbite wisdom among martial artists was if you got into a physical situation you didn't mention your training to the police. The reasoning for this was your training could be used against you (e.g., the prosecutor alleging you were looking to test your skills).

Times have changed, legal strategies have changed, and well-rounded self-defense training helps you keep up with those changes.

To this day soundbite self-defense training can be used by the prosecutor to convince the jury you were looking for trouble. At the same time well rounded—and documented training demonstrates *that wasn't the case.* Putting that in legal argle-bargle: It supports your contention that yours was a reasonable use of force decision based on an objective assessment of the circumstances. In layman's terms, you did what you had to do to stop the threat.

Documentation goes hand in hand with the terms you use in your videoed statement. If you ever find yourself in court with this evidence being admitted, any attorney worth his salt can argue that the jury should have the same education you had leading up to the fateful incident. That means introducing all kinds of evidence on your behalf. That's not just your pre-existing knowledge. It's training the jurors *with the same information* you had so they can learn it for themselves. That tends to put them on your side. This also means the jury can judge your actions, knowing what you knew at the time of that incident.

We're always told that we will face a jury of our peers. On this we call BS. Partly because we know about *voir dire*. Attorneys will excuse members of the jury pool they believe won't support their positions. The defense will excuse any potential juror they believe will be prejudiced against you while the prosecutor will weed out those who they believe would be sympathetic to you. If there is *any* chance that someone in the jury pool has any inkling of what self-defense actually looks like, they will be tossed faster than a salad. This will leave you with a jury of people who learned everything they think they know about self-defense from watching stuntmen make impossible shots while hanging off the backs of speeding motorcycles.

We've all heard the story about the guy who learned about the '21 Foot rule' while he was sitting in jail, waiting for his trial for murder. When his day in court arrived, he got on the stand and proclaimed that he shot that man in self-defense, and the '21 Foot rule' was why he acted the way he did. That was great until the prosecutor cross-examined him and asked when he learned this information. His answer was he heard about it after the incident. That earned him a one-way trip… to prison.

In one of their classes, Jenna and Jeff run their own version with students of the Tueller Drill. They time students drawing and firing two shots at a target and take an average after several tries. Then they see how far Jeff can run in the average time. (Jeff is used because he's a big, strong guy and Jenna is well... not. It's more realistic that way.) They also record all kinds of factors that could affect the process. (The weather conditions, type of gun, holster, clothing, and other pertinent information.) This is documented on certificates for students to include in their training records. If students ever need to prove they knew about this information ahead of time, they have solid records to do just that. Pre-existing knowledge anyone? With a side dish of production of evidence?

It is important to note that Jenna and Jeff timed each other drawing and shooting. Jeff was able to cover about forty-three feet in the time it took Jenna to pull her subcompact from concealment and get two shots off. Yep, you read that right. Forty-three feet in the average time it took for Jenna to get two shots on target. This was while wearing winter clothing with a gun carried on the body. Does this sound like something you might want to know? It can help you to understand you may already be behind the curve by the time you see him attacking. (When it comes to robberies drawing when you're looking down the barrel of a gun is suicidal). This is why we recommend you spend more time learning about how violence works so you have a better chance to avoid it rather than trying to be the fastest draw in the west. Guns are good tools to have, but you must earn your draw.

How will this bode for you if you truly acted in self-defense? Thinking ahead if you've properly documented your training wouldn't it be nice to have your instructors available to deliver testimony on your behalf as expert witnesses? We think so. But you will have to have acted according to your training, and your instructor has to know what he or she is talking about for this to work.

Safety isn't a list of do's and don'ts. It is a way of thinking. You're not born with this ability. It's like formal logic you need to learn to think this way, and then practice. It's also based on a foundation of reliable knowledge about danger and countermeasures. You don't have to think this way all the time, but you need the ability to shift gears into this kind of thought process when circumstances warrant it.

Afterword

We did not write this book to preach to you or to sell you our ultimate training systems. We wrote it because we've seen first hand how the holes that exist in self-defense training can get people maimed, killed, or sent to prison. We're extremely passionate about helping others get home safely to their families—no matter where they are in their self-defense journey. And we call it a journey because no one is ever really done learning about self-defense.

Here's something you've probably never heard before. The largest component of self-defense is *people skills*. Those are something you can apply in every aspect of your life. (In case you missed it these skills fall under mental preparation.) People skills are important since they do wonders to keep others from trying to drive your nose through the back of your skull or shooting you in the face. Criminals and sociopathic monsters are rare, but the world is full of folks who will attack you for pissing them off.

Getting back to self-defense and training. Our hope is that by reading this you have a better understanding of where you need to take your training. What's your next step? Next three steps? It's important to look ahead as you evaluate where you have been and what you have already learned to determine where you'll go next. But there's a practical application, too. As Jenna says, *You can't dabble in lethal force self-defense.* That's a good attitude to have—especially with any kind of weapons training.

In closing we'd like to leave you with three ideas:

- Reread
- Run

- Integrate

Reread this book in a few months to see how your understanding has changed. We've dumped a lot of information on you in a short time. And it will take time to process. When you come back to this book, you should see things in a different light—including what you missed before. In fact, give this book to training partners so you can have the thoughts from a second or third set of eyes. This will give you the framework to discuss and work on these things together. You may have different perspectives and ideas on how to implement these training ideas.

Run your previous training past this new knowledge and see where it fits—if at all. Remember we talked about the rules of engagement? Remember Marc's story about the neck break? The black belts in that class had no idea why Marc was having kittens about the technique being shown by the instructor. Knowing what you know now, review every technique in your toolbox and when you could justify its use. Do it before you actually break someone who doesn't need to be. Or try to tickle someone who needs to be broken.

Integrate your old training into the big picture of self-defense. There are many benefits, but we'll give you two examples. One is how integration can help avoid the freeze. We've given you tools to reduce freezing by helping you avoid 'analysis paralysis.' That's the common term for having so many techniques you don't know which one to use in a situation. With fast threat assessment—options that won't work are *automatically* off the table. You can get to what *will* work faster. Having immediate access to something that works to handle the situation greatly reduces your chances of freezing.

Another example is knowing what you have in your toolbox that won't work to handle the situation. When nothing you have in your toolbox would be enough—turn and go *the other way*. And do it without hesitation or shame.

We hope we've provided you with an understanding of what you need to consider about self-defense training that will keep you out of the prison showers or the ground. Remember your goal is to get safely home to your family.

Jenna and Marc

Reading List

- *101 Safety and Self-Defense Tips,* Alain Burrese
- *Aftermath: Lessons in self-defense: What to expect when the shooting stops,* Jim Fleming
- *Armed and Female*, Paxton Quigley
- *A Time To Kill: The Myth of Christian Pacifism,* Greg Hopkins
- *Beyond the Picket Fence*, Marc MacYoung
- *Big Bloody Book of Violence,* Lawrence Kane and Chris Wilder
- *Brutal Art of Ripping, Poking & Pressing Vital Targets*, Loren Christensen
- *Campfire Tales From Hell,* MacYoung/Miller/et al
- *Calling the Shots*, Jenna Meek
- *Concealed Carry for Women*, Gila Hayes
- *Conflict Communication,* Rory Miller
- *Deadly Force: Understanding Your Right to Self-Defense,* Massad Ayoob
- *Dirty Ground: The tricky space between sport and combat,* Kane and Wilder
- *Dry Fire Primer*, Annette Evans
- *Effective Defense: The Woman, The Plan, The Gun,* Hayes
- *Facing Violence,* Miller
- *Fighting in the Clinch,* Christensen
- *Fighting the Pain Resistant Attacker*, Christensen
- *Fighting Smarter: A Practical Guide for Surviving Violent Confrontations*, Tom Givens
- *Force Decisions,* Miller
- *Freedom from Fear,* Peyton Quinn
- *FTW Self-Defense*, Clint Jahn
- *Gift of Fear,* Gavin deBecker

- *… Gun Owner's Guides*, Alan Korwin
- *In the Gravest Extreme,* Ayoob
- *In the Name of Self-Defense, MacYoung*
- *Law of Self-Defense Third Edition,* Andrew Branca
- *Left of Bang,* Patrick Van Horne and Jason A. Riley
  Little Black Book of Violence, Kane and Wilder
- *Logic of Violence,* Miller
- *Manwatching*, Desmond Morris
- *Martial Arts, Self-Defense, and a Whole Lot More,* Wim Demeere
- *Meditations on Violence,* Miller
- *Multiple Attackers* (PDF with video links), MacYoung
- *On Combat,* Christensen and Dave Grossman
- *On Killing,* Grossman
- *Peoplewatching,* Morris
- *Principles Based Self-Defense Instruction*, Miller
- *Real Fighting*, Quinn
- *Saps, Jacks, and Pocket Sticks,* Terry Trahan
- *Self-Defense Against A Dog Attack*, Christensen
- *Scaling Force,* Miller
- *Straight Talk on Armed Defense,* Ayoob
- *Survive A Shooting* (active shooter), Burrese
- *Surviving Armed Assaults,* Kane and Wilder
- *Surviving a School Shooting*, Christensen
- *Surviving Workplace Violence,* Christensen
- *Timing In The Fighting Arts*, Christensen and Demeere
- *Turning Fear Into Power,* Bill Kipp
- *Why Me? The question asked by all crime victims*, Robert Bryan
- *Warriors: Living with courage, discipline, and honor*, Christensen/et al
- Warrior's Mindset, Michael Asken and Christensen
- *Writing Violence IV: Defense,* MacYoung

Tyler Tales

Tyler Story, One

Tyler is well trained in self-defense. He's spent years and thousands of dollars on training and equipment. With his emphasis on the physical, he's pretty sure he can handle himself. Tyler and his girlfriend, Brittany live on a street that ends at a park, three doors away. Late one Saturday night, they hear a disturbance in the park. Looking down the street he sees two groups facing off. He decides to go break up the situation. Seeing that there are about ten people, Tyler decides he better take a weapon along just in case. As he goes back in the house Brittany asks, "What's going on?" Tyler tells her he's going to the park. Brittany tells him to stay, but Tyler gets his 'toy,' sticks it in his pants and heads out to tell the groups to take their quarrel elsewhere.

Arriving at the park Tyler discovers two mixed groups of teenage males and females. Males from both groups have squared off and there's a confrontation between two of them. Believing his age will give him authority, Tyler demands to know what is going on. Initially they ignore him, so Tyler steps up and gets louder. Unfortunately a third guy tells Tyler to back off. Pissed off now, Tyler tells everyone he lives here and they need to leave his neighborhood. This doesn't go over well and when the kid's response has to do with Tyler's sexual practices with his mother, Tyler steps forward and shoves the younger man and demands they leave. The situation explodes into violence.

In the melee, Tyler pulls his self-defense item and uses it just as the cops roll up. Tyler and everyone else find themselves looking down the barrels of not only pistols but a rifle. Everyone is told to get down and spread their arms and legs. They lie there waiting for more police to arrive. After their arrival, everyone is immediately riot cuffed (hands zip tied together behind them) and searched. Tyler's item is taken and put into an evidence bag. When an officer interviews him, Tyler claims "self-defense." The officer asks if he left his property to come to the park. Tyler says, "Yes." Long story short, Tyler is arrested, taken to the station and charged with attempted murder. His defense bills run ten thousand dollars that he has to borrow from his parents. The lawyer gets his case pleaded down to aggravated assault. It's a slam dunk for the prosecution. Tyler spends a year in county jail and when he gets out, Brittany has left him, he has no job and he has to move back in with his parents.

To his dying day Tyler remains convinced he went to jail for defending himself.

Tyler Story, Two

Tyler has spent years training in martial arts. He even learned some decent mixed martial arts (MMA) moves. He's been repeatedly told and believes he can defend himself. One night Brittany sends him to the market. Coming out of the store, he notices three dudes following him to his car. Confident he can handle himself, he keeps walking. They speed up, and one calls out to him. Tyler stops, turns to face them, and aggressively demands, What do you want?" Two spread out from the guy in the middle who asks Tyler for money to buy beer.

Tyler refuses and adds a few insults. The speaker angrily asks, "What's your problem?" Tyler drops his groceries and takes a fighting stance. There's a blinding flash in his head on the left, and a sharp pain in his right side. Collapsing to the ground, he's beaten and robbed. The muggers flee. Tyler gets up, staggers back into the store, and the ambulance is called. He lives, but it takes months to recover from the stabbing and concussion. Tyler didn't bring a knife to a gunfight, he brought bare hands against a gang of armed robbers.

Tyler Story, Three

Tyler is a concealed carry permit holder. In his training the term "self-defense" was thrown around a lot, but never clearly defined. Tyler's running errands before meeting Brittany. Due to a long supermarket line he is running late. So he drives a little fast in the parking lot. A smaller car pulls out from behind a bigger vehicle. Despite stomping the brakes and punching the horn in warning, Tyler hits the other car. A furious Tyler jumps out of his car. So does the other driver, a guy about Tyler's age. Tempers flare, words are exchanged about who's at fault, and both try to intimidate the other to back off. The other man shoves Tyler in the chest and tells him to get out of his face. Tyler draws his gun and shoots him.

When the police arrive, Tyler claims he acted in self-defense. He shot the guy because he was “in fear for his life.” Tyler contends the guy was closing in to attack. Eye witnesses and video footage of the incident don’t support that interpretation. In fact, they tell a completely different story.

Tyler is arrested for murder and ends up taking a manslaughter plea. This time, Tyler brought a gun to a fist fight.

Tyler Story, Four

It’s Christmas Eve. Tyler and Brittany are at the home of her divorced mom. But there’s a potential hitch because Tyler and Brittany’s brother Braden have an antagonistic history. Braden, a roofer, has had a bad break-up and is staying with Mom until he gets back on his feet. Fortunately Braden is at dad’s so everyone is in high spirits and having a good time. Then Braden walks in. It’s clear he and dad were into the eggnog. He’s back home because he and dad got into an argument.

Braden starts drinking again and begins to hurl insults. Tyler initially tells him to calm down. For the sake of the family, he suggests a truce even if it is just for the evening. This pisses off Braden, and he swings at Tyler, who quickly backs away. Braden tries to hit him again, and Tyler punches him. Braden charges and tackles Tyler. Landing badly, Tyler hits his head and is momentarily stunned. In his drunken rage, Braden kneels on top of Tyler and starts to strangle him. The women try to pull him off, but he’s too strong. His air cut off, Tyler goes into survival mode, pulls his pocket knife, and stabs Braden. The knife misses Braden’s arm and goes into his chest. The paramedics are called, but Braden dies en route to the hospital.

Tyler tries to explain that he panicked because he couldn’t breathe. It’s the best description he can find, but the word panic doesn’t go over well. Tyler was correct in recognizing his life was in danger but couldn’t explain why the circumstances were life-threatening. Instead it sounds like he freaked out. The investigating officer keeps referring to the entire incident as a “fight.” Tyler doesn’t correct him.

What Tyler doesn’t know is that the DA has been told in a phone call an edited version of events and has ordered Tyler arrested. From that moment on, all the questions Tyler is asked by the police are aimed at building the state’s case and undermining his claim of self-defense.

Tyler is charged with murder one. Sure that he acted in self-defense, Tyler refuses to take a plea. Given the history between Tyler and Braden, the prosecution argues premeditation. The state continually refers to the incident as a fight and argues that lethal force was not justified. Tyler was unable to articulate that being choked while on the ground was different from fighting and rolling around. He is convicted and sent to prison.

Tyler Story, Five

Remember Tyler story one? The fight in the park? This time Tyler looks down the street, whips out his cell phone, calls the cops, reports the problem, and goes back inside to watch TV with Brittany.

Tyler Story, Six

In story three Tyler shot an unarmed man because he was adrenalized and upset. This time Tyler calmly accepts these things happen and his insurance will cover it. Remembering this he talks to the other motorist without blaming him, they exchange insurance and contact information, and Tyler goes his merry way to meet up with Brittany.

Tyler Story, Seven

At mom's house on Christmas Braden tries to get into an argument with Tyler. Instead of putting up with his abuse or arguing with a drunk, Tyler and Brittany go home.

Tyler Story, Eight

While taking the trash out Tyler sees a member of a group of young guys peeing on his lawn. Tyler shouts and begins to advance. Instead of zipping up and running (as is normal—and safe), the guy zips up and shouting insults. He and his friends advance toward Tyler. Tyler stops, pulls out his cell phone, and backs into his house while calling the police. The piddle-crew wanders off.

Tyler Story, Nine

Remember the Tyler who didn't know this stuff? He's back. He's in the parking lot after the fender bender. This time he doesn't have a gun. He's a martial artist and the other guy blows his stack and swings at Tyler. In a blaze of kung fu prowess, Tyler hits the guy hard enough to break his jaw. The man falls; Tyler leaves. Later the police show up at his home and arrest him (a parking lot video showed his license plate). He is charged with aggravated assault. Thinking he acted in self-defense, Tyler doesn't take the plea. In fact, he's told his attorney he wants to tell his story. Now he's sitting on the stand being cross-examined by the prosecutor.

Here is a list of questions the prosecutor will use to try to trip him up:

- Were you angry?
- Why didn't you leave before it got physical?
- Did you admit fault in the accident?
- Did you provoke him?
- He says you…
- The video shows you approached him did you intend to teach him a lesson?
- How did you know he was attacking?
- Why didn't you use less force?
- Don't you train to beat someone up?
- Weren't you just itchin' to use that training?
- Did you mean to maim him?
- Did you not worry about the fact you had maimed a man?
- Why'd you leave the scene?
- Isn't it true that you left because you knew you committed a crime?
- Why didn't you call the cops?
- Isn't it true that you felt good about hurting your fellow citizen?
- And many, many more...

Tyler had better have answers to these questions. Because if he fumbles on any one, the prosecutor will come in through that weakness like an attacking shark and will tear him up.

Tyler Story, Ten

Tyler's dad is in bad shape and over the years his health problems have gotten worse. Tyler moved back in with Dad to help out. Dad has never been afraid of confrontation, but over the last few months, his behavior has become more hostile and aggressive. He's also become more erratic and forgetful. Over the last two weeks Dad's been having fits of explosive rage over small things and has become paranoid. They've seen the doctor and tests were scheduled for next week, starting Monday.

Coming home from work one day, Tyler is confronted by Dad about something missing from the garage, and he blames Tyler for taking it. Tyler goes into the garage and finds it right where it's supposed to be. Coming into the kitchen, Tyler finds his dad waiting for him with a chef's knife. Screaming that he knew Tyler took it, Dad attacks. Tyler dodges the initial charge and pulls his concealed carry pistol. Unfortunately his first evasion takes him away from an easy escape route. He screams at Dad to stop, but Dad rushes at him again. Tyler shoots twice. Dad collapses. Tyler holsters his gun, kicks the knife away, pulls out his cell phone, and calls 9-1-1 before trying to stop the bleeding. Dad dies en route to the hospital.

Tyler calls his attorney who agrees to meet him at the station. Cops arrive and start asking questions. Tyler tells them he'll answer but knowing how serious this is he'll do it after he consults with his attorney and only in the presence of his attorney. Tyler is taken to the station where he waits in a cell for a few hours. He takes the time to calm down and review what happened. When his attorney arrives, Tyler consults with her in a private room without cameras. They agree that what he did was self-defense.

Later in a room with video, the detective starts asking questions:

- What happened?
- What happened to make you think you were in danger?
- How did you know that was dangerous?
- How do you explain shooting a man who only had a knife?
- Could you have used less force?

Tyler tells the whole story. He explains the living circumstances and tells them Dad became more erratic and hostile. He explains tests were scheduled but were supposed to be conducted next week. He said he had just come home, and how he'd tried to placate his father by finding the item—then things exploded. Tyler explains he has a concealed carry permit and that he was in danger because he recognized the presence of ability, opportunity, and jeopardy of the situation. He told the detective how he knew the circumstances of someone acting erratically and increasingly violently toward him, armed with a knife, and closing the distance between them meant he was about to be stabbed. Tyler stated that such an attacker could close and fatally wound him in a matter of seconds. Because it was his father didn't mean the danger wasn't real. He added escape was an unrealistic option because of the way they were positioned after the first attack. Tyler explains how he stopped shooting when Dad collapsed, called 9-1-1, and started trying to save him.

Tyler was able to articulate all of these different things to the detective and was on video telling what happened. His lawyer spotted trick questions and asked the officer to reframe them. Tyler wasn't arrested that night, was released, and told further investigation was pending.

The evidence at the scene matches Tyler's story. Other elements of his story are verified (work hours, doctor's appointments, and other aspects of the case). His articulation goes into the initial report and influences further investigation. The autopsy later reveals that his dad had a brain tumor. The undetected tumor was the cause of his dangerous behavior. Tyler is never charged.

Meet the Authors

Marc MacYoung has over twenty-five books and videos about crime, violence, and personal safety. In his youth he had the street name "Animal" and lived up to it—with all that implies. Turning his life around, he started protecting people (which got him shot at more times than when he was a thug). He's taught civilians, police, and military on three continents. He also is a court-recognized expert witness on self-defense, violence reconstruction, and knife use. Yes he is paid to talk to lawyers. The downside is he has to talk to lawyers. For more about Marc visit his website at www.NoNonsenseSelfDefense.com.

Jenna, once described as a cross between Rambo and Martha Stewart, is the author of *Calling the Shots: Self-Protection and Firearm Choices that Work for You* and a certified firearms and use of deadly force instructor. Along with her husband Jeff, she runs Carry On Colorado. When she's not writing, teaching grown-ups, or homeschooling her kiddo, she's raising chickens and getting slobbered on by her loving pack of dogs. For more about Jenna visit her training website at www.CarryOnColorado.com.

Both live and teach between Denver and Colorado Springs.

Made in the USA
Coppell, TX
26 March 2021

52405388R00115